The Canterv...
Funny Stor, ... Learn German &
Expand Your Vocabulary
the Easy Way
- With the L-R-Method

German - English Bilingual Book

by

Oscar Wilde

German Translation
Franz Blei

See the end of the book for information on a free audiobook and other bonus material.

Impressum:

Englisches Original: Oscar Wilde

Deutsche Übersetzung: Franz Blei

Der Originaltext und die Übersetzung sind gemeinfrei. Die Rechte für die zweisprachigen Ausgabe, der leicht überarbeiteten deutschen Übersetzung und der einführenden Kapitel liegen bei:

Beate Ziebell, Schillerstr.94, 15738 Zeuthen

forum-sprachen-lernen.com

info@forum-sprachen-lernen.com

Herstellung und Druck: Siehe Eindruck auf der letzten Seite

ISBN: 9781720033622

Umschlaggestaltung: Beate Ziebell

Introduction

About the creation of these books

A few years ago, I became passionately interested in learning Italian and later French. I was already fluent in English (as a native German speaker), but despite many years of school lessons, I failed in my attempt to learn Russian. Yet even a language as close to German as English, however, I had only really learned after completing school.

With a demanding job and being a single mother, spending hours at school wasn't an option. Moreover, I had also had negative experiences in school in this respect, of course. My son was learning English and French at school. I wanted to convey the experience of speaking a foreign language as being an enrichment. This skill is not only indispensable for careers today, but also opens doors to other cultures!

I was short on time but highly motivated to tackle the problem. There had to be another way of learning languages! One that was easier, faster, more sustainable. How do the best in this field manage to succeed in learning a foreign language, anyway?

These people usually practice quite a "normal" profession and still manage to learn a lot of languages on the side. They don't have much time to learn the foreign language, unlike someone who is dealing with it all day due to their job or even studying the language (such as English). I wanted to learn more about their methods.

One of these methods is the L-R method, which I will describe in greater detail later in the book. I made my first attempts to implement this method when I was looking to support my son learning English. We love the Star Trek series. I turned on the subtitles while watching it and wrote down some lines of dialog. At the same time, I recorded the soundtrack on (back then) a cassette. As a follow-up, we'd always listen to Star Trek at breakfast time. It was great for the learning process – we knew the storyline, my son loved the show and due to the repetitions on the cassette we soon had learned many passages by heart. However, over time, writing down the subtitles proved to be too time-consuming a task in the long run.

I wanted to use the same procedure in French, but in this case, it worked less well. The reason for this was that the French subtitles had very little to do with the spoken French dubbing. You can express the same thing in two very different ways; at least this was the case with the series we tried it with.

And that's how the idea for these books came about. The goal was to identify an exciting text, provide the suitable translation and an audiobook so that the spoken and written word match precisely. What's more, the text and translation should be combined in such a way that the translation can be located particularly quickly. We ultimately ended up listening to "The Red-Headed League", a Sherlock Holmes story. We love Sir Arthur Conan Doyle's language and although it's now several years ago, we still know some passages by heart.

This book is thus the result of our journey in search of good learning material and the right methods for learning languages.

Get ready to be taken into the world of Oscar Wilde, learn German at the same time and benefit from the tricks of the best in this field!

Table of Contents

See the end of the book for information on a free audiobook and other bonus material.

Dear readers!

This book can be used in many ways. On the one hand, you can sit back and relax, read German and, from time to time, let your eyes wander to the translation and brush up your German this way. In this case, you can skip the upcoming chapters about tips for quickly building up your vocabulary, the L-R method and those with many more tips.

Alternately, you can first get an initial overview of the proposed learning methods for effective language learning and the variety of bonus material offered with this book. Try the techniques! You'll be surprised how quickly your reading and listening skills will improve!

What is the quickest way to develop vocabulary?

The L-R Method

As mentioned in the introduction, in order to learn a language, you don't need much more than an interesting text, an easily identifiable suitable translation and an audiobook to learn a language.

Some people who use this method

In her book "How I Learn Languages", Kató Lomp,[1] a Hungarian translator and interpreter who was fluent in 16 languages, described how she quickly expanded her vocabulary by reading foreign-language texts. She didn't even use bilingual editions but translated unfamiliar words using a dictionary.

Phi-Staszek, a Polish multilinguist, improved this method and in the forum "How Do I Learn Any Language" described how you can learn a foreign language within a very short amount of time by only using a bilingual text and an audio recording. He referred to this method as the "L-R method". L-R stands for "Listening-Reading".

---

1   https://de.wikipedia.org/wiki/Kató_Lomb

The American linguist Stephen Krashen[2] describes **extensive reading[3] as the most effective means of language acquisition** and published many articles on the subject. Extensive reading means a lot of reading in a foreign language. With this method, it's not important to understand every word, but to follow the story and find out what happens next. The enjoyment of reading is paramount.

The Oxford University Press ELT also published an article on this topic. It showed that EFL[4] students who **read** a lot do not only learn to read a foreign language **fluently**, but also improve their writing skills in the respective language. According to the study, extensive reading also led to **improved listening skills** and even to a **better active vocabulary**, meaning better speaking skills in the foreign language.

All good reasons for embracing extensive reading and the L-R method!

A practical approach to the L-R method

If an audiobook exists, extensive reading can be more effectively applied to learn a foreign language with the L-R method. Here is the approach for how to learn a great deal within as little time as possible:

1. **First, read the translation** to familiarise yourself with the content of the text. Depending on previous knowledge, this can be one page or maybe even several pages.
2. **Next, listen to the book version and read it in German** at the same time. Try to understand every word and read at the same time. If you can understand everything and read along easily, you can move on to point
3. **Listening without reading**. Maybe even close your eyes. Can you still understand everything? If so, then you can move on to point 4. If not, briefly stop at the places you do not yet understand and look up the unfamiliar word.
4. **Now that you understand the text blindly**, you can **switch to passive listening**. Take the audiobook and listen to it again and again. Set your MP3 player to "repeat indefinitely". It won't hurt to

---

2   https://de.wikipedia.org/wiki/Stephen_Krashen
3   https://oupeltglobalblog.com/2017/01/11/extensive-reading-and-language-learning/
4   EFL= English as a Foreign Language

listen to the whole story over and over again. Then you have already prepared yourself for the next sections and will be faster at points 1 to 3. You will notice that you will soon know many sentences of the text by heart.

Why does the method work?

The amount of text

By reading extensively, you will learn a vast amount of German vocabulary, a plethora of sentence constructions and also, indirectly, about grammar.

Here's an example: Suppose you divide the book "The Red-Headed League" into 30 sections (one section accounts for about 1.5 pages or two minutes of the audiobook). The process of actively going through a part, i.e. the time you actually spend on working out the text with the help of book and audiobook (points 1 to 3 of the L-R method), will not take much longer than 20 minutes (this may take a little longer if there is little or no previous knowledge).

With the commitment of 20 minutes a day, you've worked your way through the entire vocabulary of the Sherlock Holmes story after 30 days, and that's about 1800 different words! Reading can only be learned by reading and this also applies to reading a foreign language. The audiobook contributes to the improvement of listening comprehension and pronunciation.

The layout of the text

By allocating the foreign language to the translation sentence by sentence, the meaning of unknown words can be grasped particularly quickly.

Start the learning with the most common words

Did you know that with the 1000 most-used words[5] of a language you can already understand 76 per cent of a novel's content and about 90 per cent of the spoken language? This was the result of a study by Mark Davies[6]. The percentage varies somewhat from one language to another, but it's an encouraging trend nevertheless. Encouraging because, as shown above, 1000 words can be learned quite fast. This then allows you to move on to content that suits your interests sooner. The meaning of many other words then become apparent from the context without you needing a dictionary.

For this purpose, this book offers a free Anki[7] deck as bonus material for learning the most important German words from various subject areas. Anki is software that is used for the acquisition of vocabulary and other facts. It's free, except for iPhones (it costs about 20 euros to use it on an iPhone). Anki uses its temporal repetition algorithm to ensure that the vocabulary is increasingly anchored in the long-term memory. The "Anki deck" is the name of the different facts to be learned.

Tips for using the Anki deck:

- Learn whole sentences.
- Focus on understanding the word in context (meaning, focus on the extension of the passive vocabulary).
- Take advantage of every opportunity to learn, for example when queuing or commuting to work.

Why learn whole sentences?

A single word can have many meanings. Mark Twain formulated this very aptly in his book "The Awful German Language" with the help of the word "Zug":
Zug: Strictly speaking, "Zug" means: jerk, tug, air flow, procession, march, advance, birds' flight, direction, campaign, railroad, caravan, etc. The real

---

5   http://www.lingref.com/cpp/hls/7/paper1091.pdf
6   http://howlearnspanish.com/2010/08/how-many-words-do-you-need-to-know/
7   https://apps.ankiweb.net/

meaning of "Zug" can thus only be deducted through the context.

For this reason, the deck is not made up of individual terms, but mostly of entire sentences. To read the dialogues, a book in PDF format is available. In the book, there are also gaps to complete as well as their solutions to deepen the knowledge. The Foreign Service Institute created the dialogues. They were drafted for American diplomats who needed to get a handle on the respective country's language as quickly as possible before their stay abroad. If sentences aren't relevant to you, don't hesitate to delete them. Focus on the vocabulary that's important to you. The partially literal translation is particularly positive.

Why should you focus on passive learning?

Again, this is about the amount of vocabulary that you can learn. Adding a word to your passive vocabulary is much faster than adding it to the active vocabulary.

Thus, it's quite possible to increase one's passive vocabulary by a significant amount every day. In contrast, it would only be possible to expand the active vocabulary by a few terms. How much that precisely is, undoubtedly varies from one person to another.

As a general rule, however, the following applies: it is substantially easier to expand the passive vocabulary than it is to develop the active one. The higher the passive vocabulary, the more quickly, and more comprehensively you will be able to read other content. The more time you spend with the foreign language, the greater the extent of your automatic active vocabulary improvement will be. And with this method, you'll do so even faster!

Chapter 1

When Mr. Hiram B. Otis, the American Minister, bought Canterville Chase, every one told him he was doing a very foolish thing, as there was no doubt at all that the place was haunted.

Indeed, Lord Canterville himself, who was a man of the most punctilious honour, had felt it his duty to mention the fact to Mr. Otis when they came to discuss terms.

"We have not cared to live in the place ourselves," said Lord Canterville, "since my grandaunt, the Dowager Duchess of Bolton, was frightened into a fit, from which she never really recovered, by two skeleton hands being placed on her shoulders as she was dressing for dinner,

and I feel bound to tell you, Mr. Otis, that the ghost has been seen by several living members of my family, as well as by the rector of the parish, the Rev. Augustus Dampier, who is a Fellow of King's College, Cambridge.

After the unfortunate accident to the Duchess, none of our younger servants would stay with us, and Lady Canterville often got very little sleep at night, in consequence of the mysterious noises that came from the corridor and the library."

"My Lord," answered the Minister, "I will take the furniture and the ghost at a valuation.

I have come from a modern country, where we have everything that money

Als Mr. Hiram B. Otis, der amerikanische Gesandte, Schloss Canterville kaufte, sagte ihm ein jeder, dass er sehr töricht daran täte, da dieses Schloss ohne Zweifel verwünscht sei.

Sogar Lord Canterville selbst, ein Mann von peinlichster Ehrlichkeit, hatte es als seine Pflicht betrachtet, diese Tatsache Mr. Otis mitzuteilen, bevor sie den Verkauf abschlossen.

„Wir haben selbst nicht in dem Schloss gewohnt", sagte Lord Canterville, „seit meine Großtante, die Herzogin-Mutter von Bolton, einst vor Schreck in Krämpfe verfiel, von denen sie sich nie wieder erholte, weil ein Skelett seine beiden Hände ihr auf die Schultern legte, als sie gerade beim Ankleiden war.

Ich fühle mich verpflichtet, es Ihnen zu sagen, Mr. Otis, dass der Geist noch jetzt von verschiedenen Mitgliedern der Familie Canterville gesehen worden ist, sowie auch vom Geistlichen unserer Gemeinde, Hochwürden Augustus Dampier, der in King's College, Cambridge, den Doktor gemacht hat.

Nach dem Malheur mit der Herzogin wollte keiner unserer Dienstboten mehr bei uns bleiben, und Lady Canterville konnte seitdem des Nachts häufig nicht mehr schlafen vor lauter unheimlichen Geräuschen, die vom Korridor und von der Bibliothek herkamen."

„Mylord", antwortete der Gesandte, „ich will die ganze Einrichtung und den Geist dazu kaufen.

Ich komme aus einem modernen Land, wo wir alles haben, was mit Geld zu

can buy; and with all our spry young fellows painting the Old World red, and carrying off your best actors and prima-donnas, I reckon that if there were such a thing as a ghost in Europe, we'd have it at home in a very short time in one of our public museums, or on the road as a show."

"I fear that the ghost exists," said Lord Canterville, smiling, "though it may have resisted the overtures of your enterprising impresarios.

It has been well known for three centuries, since 1584 in fact, and always makes its appearance before the death of any member of our family."

"Well, so does the family doctor for that matter, Lord Canterville.

But there is no such thing, sir, as a ghost, and I guess the laws of Nature are not going to be suspended for the British aristocracy."

"You are certainly very natural in America," answered Lord Canterville, who did not quite understand Mr. Otis's last observation, "and if you don't mind a ghost in the house, it is all right.

Only you must remember I warned you."

A few weeks after this, the purchase was concluded, and at the close of the season the Minister and his family went down to Canterville Chase.

Mrs. Otis, who, as Miss Lucretia R. Tappan, of West 53d Street, had been a celebrated New York belle, was now a very handsome, middle-aged woman, with fine eyes, and a superb profile.

Many American ladies on leaving their

native land adopt an appearance of chronic ill-health, under the impression that it is a form of European refinement, but Mrs. Otis had never fallen into this error.

She had a magnificent constitution, and a really wonderful amount of animal spirits.

Indeed, in many respects, she was quite English, and was an excellent example of the fact that we have really everything in common with America nowadays, except, of course, language.

Her eldest son, christened Washington by his parents in a moment of patriotism, which he never ceased to regret, was a fair-haired, rather good-looking young man, who had qualified himself for American diplomacy by leading the German at the Newport Casino for three successive seasons, and even in London was well known as an excellent dancer.

Gardenias and the peerage were his only weaknesses.

Otherwise he was extremely sensible.

Miss Virginia E. Otis was a little girl of fifteen, lithe and lovely as a fawn, and with a fine freedom in her large blue eyes.

She was a wonderful Amazon, and had once raced old Lord Bilton on her pony twice round the park, winning by a length and a half, just in front of the Achilles statue, to the huge delight of the young Duke of Cheshire, who proposed for her on the spot, and was sent back to Eton that very night by his guardians, in floods of tears.

verlassen, nehmen mit der Zeit das Gebaren einer chronischen Kränklichkeit an, da sie dies für ein Zeichen europäischer Kultur ansehen; aber Mrs. Otis war nie in diesen Irrtum verfallen.

Sie besaß eine vortreffliche Konstitution und einen hervorragenden Unternehmungsgeist.

So war sie wirklich in vieler Hinsicht völlig englisch und ein vorzügliches Beispiel für die Tatsache, dass wir heutzutage alles mit Amerika gemein haben, ausgenommen natürlich die Sprache.

Ihr ältester Sohn, den die Eltern in einem heftigen Anfall von Patriotismus Washington genannt hatten, was er zeit seines Lebens beklagte, war ein blonder, hübscher junger Mann, der sich dadurch für den diplomatischen Dienst geeignet gezeigt hatte, dass er im Newport Casino während dreier Winter die Françaisen kommandierte und sogar in London als vorzüglicher Tänzer galt.

Gardenien und der Adelskalender waren seine einzigen Schwächen.

Im Übrigen war er außerordentlich vernünftig.

Miss Virginia E. Otis war ein kleines Fräulein von fünfzehn Jahren, graziös und lieblich wie ein junges Reh und mit schönen, klaren blauen Augen.

Sie saß brillant zu Pferde und hatte einmal auf ihrem Pony mit dem alten Lord Bilton ein Wettrennen um den Park veranstaltet, wobei sie mit 1 1/2 Pferdelängen Siegerin geblieben war, gerade vor der Achillesstatue, zum ganz besonderen Entzücken des jungen Herzogs von Cheshire, der sofort um ihre Hand anhielt und noch denselben Abend unter Strömen von Tränen nach Eton in seine Schule zurückgeschickt wurde.

After Virginia came the twins, who were usually called "The Star and Stripes," as they were always getting swished.

They were delightful boys, and, with the exception of the worthy Minister, the only true republicans of the family.

As Canterville Chase is seven miles from Ascot, the nearest railway station, Mr. Otis had telegraphed for a waggonette to meet them, and they started on their drive in high spirits.

It was a lovely July evening, and the air was delicate with the scent of the pinewoods.

Now and then they heard a wood-pigeon brooding over its own sweet voice, or saw, deep in the rustling fern, the burnished breast of the pheasant.

Little squirrels peered at them from the beech-trees as they went by, and the rabbits scudded away through the brushwood and over the mossy knolls, with their white tails in the air.

As they entered the avenue of Canterville Chase, however, the sky became suddenly overcast with clouds, a curious stillness seemed to hold the atmosphere, a great flight of rooks passed silently over their heads, and, before they reached the house, some big drops of rain had fallen.

Standing on the steps to receive them was an old woman, neatly dressed in black silk, with a white cap and apron. This was Mrs. Umney, the housekeeper, whom Mrs. Otis, at Lady Canterville's earnest request, had consented to keep in her former position.

She made them each a low curtsey as they alighted, and said in a quaint, old-fashioned manner, "I bid you welcome

Nach Virginia kamen die Zwillinge, die gewöhnlich „Stars and Stripes" genannt wurden, da sie immer durchgeprügelt wurden.

Es waren entzückende Buben, die in der Familie, mit Ausnahme des Herrn vom Hause natürlich, die einzigen wirklichen Republikaner waren.

Da Schloss Canterville sieben Meilen von der nächsten Eisenbahnstation Ascot entfernt liegt, hatte Mr. Otis den Wagen bestellt, sie da abzuholen, und die Familie befand sich in der heitersten Stimmung.

Es war ein herrlicher Juliabend und die Luft war voll vom frischen Duft der nahen Tannenwälder.

Ab und zu ließ sich die süße Stimme der Holztaube in der Ferne hören, und ein buntglänzender Fasan raschelte durch die hohen Farnkräuter am Wege.

Kleine Eichhörnchen blickten ihnen von den Buchen nach, als sie vorbeifuhren und die Kaninchen ergriffen die Flucht und schossen durch das Unterholz und die moosigen Hügelchen dahin, die weißen Schwänzchen hoch in der Luft.

Als man in den Park von Schloss Canterville einbog, bedeckte sich der Himmel plötzlich mit dunklen Wolken; die Luft schien gleichsam stillzustehen; ein großer Schwarm Krähen flog lautlos über ihren Häuptern dahin, und ehe man noch das Haus erreichte, fiel der Regen in dicken, schweren Tropfen.

Auf der Freitreppe empfing sie eine alte Frau in schwarzer Seide mit weißer Haube und Schürze: das war Mrs. Umney, die Wirtschafterin, die Mrs. Otis auf Lady Cantervilles inständiges Bitten in ihrer bisherigen Stellung behalten wollte.

Sie machte jedem einen tiefen Knicks, als sie nacheinander ausstiegen und sagte in einer eigentümlich

to Canterville Chase."

Following her, they passed through the fine Tudor hall into the library, a long, low room, panelled in black oak, at the end of which was a large stained glass window.

Here they found tea laid out for them, and, after taking off their wraps, they sat down and began to look round, while Mrs. Umney waited on them.

Suddenly Mrs. Otis caught sight of a dull red stain on the floor just by the fireplace, and, quite unconscious of what it really signified, said to Mrs. Umney, "I am afraid something has been spilt there."

"Yes, madam," replied the old housekeeper in a low voice, "blood has been spilt on that spot."

"How horrid!" cried Mrs. Otis;

"I don't at all care for blood-stains in a sitting-room.

It must be removed at once."

The old woman smiled, and answered in the same low, mysterious voice, "It is the blood of Lady Eleanore de Canterville, who was murdered on that very spot by her own husband, Sir Simon de Canterville, in 1575.

Sir Simon survived her nine years, and disappeared suddenly under very mysterious circumstances.

His body has never been discovered, but his guilty spirit still haunts the Chase.

The blood-stain has been much admired by tourists and others, and cannot be removed."

"That is all nonsense," cried Washington Otis; "Pinkerton's Champion Stain

altmodischen Art: „Ich heiße Sie auf Schloss Canterville willkommen."

Man folgte ihr ins Haus, durch die schöne alte Tudorhalle in die Bibliothek, ein langes, niedriges Zimmer mit Täfelung von schwarzem Eichenholz und einem großen bunten Glasfenster.

Hier war der Tee für die Herrschaften gerichtet; und nachdem sie sich ihrer Mäntel entledigt, setzten sie sich und sahen sich um, während Mrs. Umney sie bediente.

Da bemerkte Mrs. Otis plötzlich einen großen roten Fleck auf dem Fußboden, gerade vor dem Kamin, und in völliger Unkenntnis von dessen Bedeutung sagte sie zu Mrs. Umney: „Ich fürchte, da hat man aus Unvorsichtigkeit etwas verschüttet."

„Ja, gnädige Frau", erwiderte die alte Haushälterin leise, „auf jenem Fleck ist Blut geflossen."

„Wie grässlich!" rief Mrs. Otis.

„Ich liebe durchaus nicht Blutflecke in einem Wohnzimmer.

Er muss sofort entfernt werden."

Die alte Frau lächelte und erwiderte mit derselben leisen, geheimnisvollen Stimme: „Es ist das Blut von Lady Eleanore de Canterville, welche hier auf dieser Stelle von ihrem eigenen Gemahl, Sir Simon de Canterville, im Jahre 1575 ermordet wurde.

Sir Simon überlebte sie um neun Jahre und verschwand dann plötzlich unter ganz geheimnisvollen Umständen.

Sein Leichnam ist nie gefunden worden, aber sein schuldbeladener Geist geht noch jetzt hier im Schloss um.

Der Blutfleck wurde schon oft von Reisenden bewundert und kann durch nichts entfernt werden."

„Das ist alles Humbug", rief Washington Otis, „Pinkertons

Remover and Paragon Detergent will clean it up in no time," and before the terrified housekeeper could interfere, he had fallen upon his knees, and was rapidly scouring the floor with a small stick of what looked like a black cosmetic.

In a few moments no trace of the blood-stain could be seen.

"I knew Pinkerton would do it," he exclaimed, triumphantly, as he looked round at his admiring family; but no sooner had he said these words than a terrible flash of lightning lit up the sombre room, a fearful peal of thunder made them all start to their feet, and Mrs. Umney fainted.

"What a monstrous climate!"

said the American Minister, calmly, as he lit a long cheroot.

"I guess the old country is so overpopulated that they have not enough decent weather for everybody.

I have always been of opinion that emigration is the only thing for England."

"My dear Hiram," cried Mrs. Otis, "what can we do with a woman who faints?"

"Charge it to her like breakages," answered the Minister; "she won't faint after that;" and in a few moments Mrs. Umney certainly came to.

There was no doubt, however, that she was extremely upset, and she sternly warned Mr. Otis to beware of some trouble coming to the house.

"I have seen things with my own eyes, sir," she said, "that would make any

Universal-Fleckenreiniger wird ihn im Nu beseitigen"; und ehe noch die erschrockene Haushälterin ihn davon zurückhalten konnte, lag er schon auf den Knien und scheuerte die Stelle am Boden mit einem kleinen Stumpf von etwas, das schwarzer Bartwichse ähnlich sah.

In wenigen Augenblicken war keine Spur mehr von dem Blutfleck zu sehen.

„Na, ich wusste ja, dass Pinkerton das machen würde", rief er triumphierend, während er sich zu seiner bewundernden Familie wandte; aber kaum hatte er diese Worte gesagt, da erleuchtete ein greller Blitz das düstere Zimmer, und ein tosender Donnerschlag ließ sie alle in die Höhe fahren, während Mrs. Umney in Ohnmacht fiel.

„Was für ein schauderhaftes Klima!",

sagte der amerikanische Gesandte ruhig, während er sich eine neue Zigarette ansteckte.

„Wahrscheinlich ist dieses alte Land so übervölkert, dass sie nicht mehr genug anständiges Wetter für jeden haben.

Meiner Ansicht nach ist Auswanderung das einzig Richtige für England."

„Mein lieber Hiram", sprach Mrs. Otis, „was sollen wir bloß mit einer Frau anfangen, die ohnmächtig wird?"

„Rechne es ihr an, als ob sie etwas zerschlagen hätte, dann wird es nicht wieder vorkommen", sagte der Gesandte; und in der Tat, schon nach wenigen Augenblicken kam Mrs. Umney wieder zu sich.

Aber es war kein Zweifel, dass sie sehr aufgeregt war, und sie warnte Mr. Otis, es stände seinem Hause ein Unglück bevor.

„Ich habe mit meinen eigenen Augen Dinge gesehen, Herr", sagte sie, „dass

Christian's hair stand on end, and many and many a night I have not closed my eyes in sleep for the awful things that are done here."

Mr. Otis, however, and his wife warmly assured the honest soul that they were not afraid of ghosts, and, after invoking the blessings of Providence on her new master and mistress, and making arrangements for an increase of salary, the old housekeeper tottered off to her own room.

jedem Christenmenschen die Haare davon zu Berge stehen würden, und manche Nacht habe ich kein Auge zugetan aus Furcht vor dem Schrecklichen, das hier geschehen ist."

Jedoch Herr und Frau Otis beruhigten die ehrliche Seele, erklärten, dass sie sich nicht vor Gespenstern fürchteten, und nachdem die alte Haushälterin noch den Segen der Vorsehung auf ihre neue Herrschaft herabgefleht und um Erhöhung ihres Gehaltes gebeten hatte, schlich sie zitternd auf ihre Stube.

Chapter 2

The storm raged fiercely all that night, but nothing of particular note occurred.

Der Sturm wütete die ganze Nacht hindurch, aber sonst ereignete sich nichts von besonderer Bedeutung.

The next morning, however, when they came down to breakfast, they found the terrible stain of blood once again on the floor.

Am nächsten Morgen jedoch, als die Familie zum Frühstück herunterkam, fanden sie den fürchterlichen Blutfleck wieder unverändert auf dem Fußboden.

"I don't think it can be the fault of the Paragon Detergent," said Washington, "for I have tried it with everything. It must be the ghost."

„Ich glaube nicht, dass die Schuld hiervon an Pinkertons Fleckenreiniger liegt", erklärte Washington, „denn den habe ich immer mit Erfolg angewendet — es muss also das Gespenst sein."

He accordingly rubbed out the stain a second time, but the second morning it appeared again.

Er rieb nun zum zweiten Mal den Fleck weg, aber am nächsten Morgen war er gleichwohl wieder da.

The third morning also it was there, though the library had been locked up at night by Mr. Otis himself, and the key carried up-stairs.

Ebenso am dritten Morgen, trotzdem Mr. Otis selbst die Bibliothek am Abend vorher zugeschlossen und den Schlüssel mit nach oben genommen.

The whole family were now quite interested;

Jetzt interessierte sich die ganze Familie für die Sache.

Mr. Otis began to suspect that he had been too dogmatic in his denial of the

Mr. Otis fing an zu glauben, dass es doch allzu skeptisch von ihm gewesen

existence of ghosts,

Mrs. Otis expressed her intention of joining the Psychical Society, and Washington prepared a long letter to Messrs. Myers and Podmore on the subject of the Permanence of Sanguineous Stains when connected with Crime.

That night all doubts about the objective existence of phantasmata were removed for ever.

The day had been warm and sunny; and, in the cool of the evening, the whole family went out to drive.

They did not return home till nine o'clock, when they had a light supper.

The conversation in no way turned upon ghosts, so there were not even those primary conditions of receptive expectations which so often precede the presentation of psychical phenomena.

The subjects discussed, as I have since learned from Mr. Otis, were merely such as form the ordinary conversation of cultured Americans of the better class,

such as the immense superiority of Miss Fanny Devonport over Sarah Bernhardt as an actress; the difficulty of obtaining green corn, buckwheat cakes, and hominy, even in the best English houses; the importance of Boston in the development of the world-soul; the advantages of the baggage-check system in railway travelling; and the sweetness of the New York accent as compared to the London drawl.

No mention at all was made of the supernatural, nor was Sir Simon de

sei, die Existenz aller Gespenster zu leugnen.

Mrs. Otis sprach die Absicht aus, der Psychologischen Gesellschaft beizutreten, und Washington schrieb einen langen Brief an die Herren Myers & Podmore über die Unvertilgbarkeit blutiger Flecken im Zusammenhang mit Verbrechen.

In der darauffolgenden Nacht nun wurde jeder Zweifel an der Existenz von Gespenstern für immer endgültig beseitigt.

Den Tag über war es heiß und sonnig gewesen und in der Kühle des Abends fuhr die Familie spazieren.

Man kehrte erst gegen neun Uhr zurück, worauf das Abendessen eingenommen wurde.

Die Unterhaltung berührte in keiner Weise Gespenster; es war also nicht einmal die Grundbedingung jener erwartungsvollen Aufnahmefähigkeit gegeben, welche so oft dem Erscheinen solcher Phänomene vorangeht.

Die Gesprächsthemata waren, wie mir Mrs. Otis seitdem mitgeteilt hat, lediglich solche, wie sie unter gebildeten Amerikanern der besseren Klasse üblich sind,

wie z. B. die ungeheure Überlegenheit von Maß Fanny Datenport über Sarah Bernhard als Schauspielerin; die Schwierigkeit, Grünkern- und Buchweizenkuchen selbst in den besten englischen Häusern zu bekommen; die hohe Bedeutung von Boston in Hinsicht auf die Entwicklung der Weltseele; die Vorzüge des Freigepäcksystems beim Eisenbahnfahren; und die angenehme Weichheit des New Yorker Akzents im Gegensatz zum schleppenden Londoner Dialekt.

In keiner Weise wurde weder das Übernatürliche berührt, noch von Sir

Canterville alluded to in any way.

At eleven o'clock the family retired, and by half-past all the lights were out.

Some time after, Mr. Otis was awakened by a curious noise in the corridor, outside his room.

It sounded like the clank of metal, and seemed to be coming nearer every moment.

He got up at once, struck a match, and looked at the time.

It was exactly one o'clock.

He was quite calm, and felt his pulse, which was not at all feverish.

The strange noise still continued, and with it he heard distinctly the sound of footsteps.

He put on his slippers, took a small oblong phial out of his dressing-case, and opened the door.

Right in front of him he saw, in the wan moonlight, an old man of terrible aspect.

His eyes were as red burning coals; long grey hair fell over his shoulders in matted coils; his garments, which were of antique cut, were soiled and ragged, and from his wrists and ankles hung heavy manacles and rusty gyves.

"My dear sir," said Mr. Otis, "I really must insist on your oiling those chains, and have brought you for that purpose a small bottle of the Tammany Rising Sun Lubricator.

It is said to be completely efficacious upon one application, and there are several testimonials to that effect on the wrapper from some of our most eminent native divines.

Simon de Canterville gesprochen.

Um elf Uhr trennte man sich und eine halbe Stunde darauf war alle Lichter aus.

Da plötzlich wachte Mr. Otis von einem Geräusch auf dem Korridor vor seiner Tür auf.

Es klang wie Rasseln von Metall und schien mit jedem Augenblick näher zu kommen.

Der Gesandte stand sofort auf, zündete Licht an und sah nach der Uhr.

Es war Punkt eins.

Er war ganz ruhig und fühlte sich den Puls, der nicht im geringsten fieberhaft war.

Das sonderbare Geräusch dauerte an und er hörte deutlich Schritte.

Er zog die Pantoffel an, nahm eine längliche Phiole von seinem Toilettentisch und öffnete die Tür.

Da sah er, sich direkt gegenüber, im blassen Schein des Mondes, einen alten Mann von ganz grauslichem Aussehen stehen.

Seine Augen waren rot wie brennende Kohlen; langes graues Haar fiel in wirren Locken über seine Schultern; seine Kleidung von altmodischem Schnitt war beschmutzt und zerrissen, und schwere rostige Fesseln hingen ihm an Füßen und Händen.

„Mein lieber Herr", sagte Mr. Otis, „ich muss Sie schon bitten, Ihre Ketten etwas zu schmieren, und ich habe Ihnen zu dem Zweck hier eine kleine Flasche von Tammanys Rising Sun Lubricator mitgebracht.

Man sagt, dass schon ein einmaliger Gebrauch genügt, und auf dem Umschlag finden Sie die glänzendsten Atteste hierüber von unsern hervorragendsten einheimischen

I shall leave it here for you by the bedroom candles, and will be happy to supply you with more, should you require it."

With these words the United States Minister laid the bottle down on a marble table, and, closing his door, retired to rest.

For a moment the Canterville ghost stood quite motionless in natural indignation; then, dashing the bottle violently upon the polished floor, he fled down the corridor, uttering hollow groans, and emitting a ghastly green light.

Just, however, as he reached the top of the great oak staircase, a door was flung open, two little white-robed figures appeared, and a large pillow whizzed past his head!

There was evidently no time to be lost, so, hastily adopting the Fourth dimension of Space as a means of escape, he vanished through the wainscoting, and the house became quite quiet.

On reaching a small secret chamber in the left wing, he leaned up against a moonbeam to recover his breath, and began to try and realize his position.

Never, in a brilliant and uninterrupted career of three hundred years, had he been so grossly insulted.

He thought of the Dowager Duchess, whom he had frightened into a fit as she stood before the glass in her lace and diamonds;

of the four housemaids, who had gone into hysterics when he merely grinned

Geistlichen.

Ich werde es Ihnen hier neben das Licht stellen und bin mit Vergnügen bereit, Ihnen auf Wunsch mehr davon zu besorgen."

Mit diesen Worten stellte der Gesandte der Vereinigten Staaten das Fläschchen auf einen Marmortisch, schloss die Tür und legte sich wieder zu Bett.

Für einen Augenblick war das Gespenst von Canterville ganz starr vor Entrüstung; dann schleuderte es die Flasche wütend auf den Boden und floh den Korridor hinab, indem es ein dumpfes Stöhnen ausstieß und ein gespenstisch grünes Licht um sich verbreitete.

Als es gerade die große eichene Treppe erreichte, öffnete sich eine Tür, zwei kleine weißgekleidete Gestalten erschienen, und ein großes Kissen sauste an seinem Kopf vorbei.

Da war augenscheinlich keine Zeit zu verlieren; und indem es hastig die vierte Dimension als Mittel zur Flucht benutzte, verschwand es durch die Täfelung, worauf das Haus ruhig wurde.

Als das Gespenst ein kleines geheimes Zimmer im linken Schlossflügel erreicht hatte, lehnte es sich erschöpft gegen einen Mondstrahl, um erst wieder zu Atem zu kommen, und versuchte sich seine Lage klarzumachen.

Niemals war es in seiner glänzenden und ununterbrochenen Laufbahn von dreihundert Jahren so gröblich beleidigt worden.

Es dachte an die Herzogin-Mutter, die bei seinem Anblick Krämpfe bekommen hatte, als sie in ihren Spitzen und Diamanten vor dem Spiegel stand;

an die vier Hausmädchen, die hysterisch wurden, als es sie bloß durch die

at them through the curtains on one of the spare bedrooms; of the rector of the parish, whose candle he had blown out as he was coming late one night from the library, and who had been under the care of Sir William Gull ever since, a perfect martyr to nervous disorders;

and of old Madame de Tremouillac, who, having wakened up one morning early and seen a skeleton seated in an armchair by the fire reading her diary, had been confined to her bed for six weeks with an attack of brain fever, and, on her recovery, had become reconciled to the Church, and broken off her connection with that notorious sceptic, Monsieur de Voltaire.

He remembered the terrible night when the wicked Lord Canterville was found choking in his dressing-room, with the knave of diamonds half-way down his throat, and confessed, just before he died, that he had cheated Charles James Fox out of £50,000 at Crockford's by means of that very card, and swore that the ghost had made him swallow it.

All his great achievements came back to him again, from the butler who had shot himself in the pantry because he had seen a green hand tapping at the window-pane, to the beautiful Lady Stutfield, who was always obliged to wear a black velvet band round her throat to hide the mark of five fingers burnt upon her white skin, and who drowned herself at last in the carp-pond at the end of the King's Walk.

With the enthusiastic egotism of the true artist, he went over his most celebrated performances, and smiled bitterly to himself as he recalled to mind his last

Vorhänge eines der unbewohnten Schlafzimmer hindurch anlächelte; an den Pfarrer der Gemeinde, dessen Licht es eines Nachts ausgeblasen, als derselbe einmal spät aus der Bibliothek kam, und der seitdem beständig bei Sir William Gull, geplagt von Nervenstörungen, in Behandlung war;

an die alte Madame du Tremouillac, die, als sie eines Morgens früh aufwachte und in ihrem Lehnstuhl am Kamine ein Skelett sitzen sah, das ihr Tagebuch las, darauf sechs Wochen fest im Bett lag an der Gehirnentzündung und nach ihrer Genesung eine treue Anhängerin der Kirche wurde und jede Verbindung mit dem bekannten Freigeist Monsieur de Voltaire abbrach.

Es erinnerte sich der entsetzlichen Nacht, als der böse Lord Canterville in seinem Ankleidezimmer halb erstickt gefunden wurde mit dem Karobuben im Halse und gerade noch, ehe er starb, beichtete, dass er Charles James Fox vermittelst dieser Karte bei Crockfords um 50000 Pfund Sterling betrogen hatte und dass ihm nun das Gespenst die Karte in den Hals gesteckt habe.

Alle seine großen Taten kamen ihm ins Gedächtnis zurück, von dem Kammerdiener an, der sich in der Kirche erschoss, weil es eine grüne Hand hatte an die Scheiben klopfen sehen, bis zu der schönen Lady Stutfield, die immer ein schwarzes Samtband um den Hals tragen musste, damit die Spur von fünf in ihre weiße Haut eingebrannten Fingern verdeckt wurde, und die sich schließlich in dem Karpfenteich am Ende der Königspromenade ertränkte.

Mit dem begeisterten Egoismus des echten Künstlers versetzte es sich im Geiste wieder in seine hervorragendsten Rollen und lächelte bitter, als es an sein

appearance as "Red Reuben, or the Strangled Babe," his début as "Guant Gibeon, the Blood-sucker of Bexley Moor," and the furore he had excited one lovely June evening by merely playing ninepins with his own bones upon the lawn-tennis ground.

And after all this some wretched modern Americans were to come and offer him the Rising Sun Lubricator, and throw pillows at his head!

It was quite unbearable.

Besides, no ghost in history had ever been treated in this manner.

Accordingly, he determined to have vengeance, and remained till daylight in an attitude of deep thought.

letztes Auftreten als ‚Roter Ruben oder das erwürgte Kind' dachte, oder sein Debüt als ‚Riese Gibeon, der Blutsauger von Bexley Moor', und das Furore, das es eines schönen Juliabends gemacht hatte, als es ganz einfach auf dem Tennisplatz mit seinen eigenen Knochen Kegel spielte.

Und nach alledem kommen solche elenden modernen Amerikaner, bieten ihm Rising Sun-Öl an und werfen ihm Kissen an den Kopf!

Es war nicht auszuhalten.

So war noch niemals in der Weltgeschichte ein Gespenst behandelt worden.

Es schwor demgemäß Rache und blieb bis Tagesanbruch in tiefe Gedanken versunken.

Chapter 3

The next morning, when the Otis family met at breakfast, they discussed the ghost at some length.

The United States Minister was naturally a little annoyed to find that his present had not been accepted.

"I have no wish," he said, "to do the ghost any personal injury, and I must say that, considering the length of time he has been in the house, I don't think it is at all polite to throw pillows at him,"--a very just remark, at which, I am sorry to say, the twins burst into shouts of laughter.

Als am nächsten Morgen die Familie Otis zum Frühstück zusammenkam, wurde das Gespenst natürlich des längeren besprochen.

Der Gesandte der Vereinigten Staaten war selbstverständlich etwas ungehalten, dass sein Geschenk so missachtet worden war.

„Ich habe durchaus nicht die Absicht", erklärte er, „dem Geist irgendeine persönliche Beleidigung zuzufügen, und ich muss sagen, dass es aus Rücksicht auf die lange Zeit, die er nun schon hier im Hause wohnt, nicht höflich ist, ihn mit Kissen zu bewerfen" — eine sehr wohlangebrachte Bemerkung, bei welcher, wie ich leider gestehen muss, die Zwillinge in ein lautes Gelächter ausbrachen.

"Upon the other hand," he continued, "if he really declines to use the Rising Sun Lubricator, we shall have to take his chains from him. It would be quite impossible to sleep, with such a noise going on outside the bedrooms."

For the rest of the week, however, they were undisturbed, the only thing that excited any attention being the continual renewal of the blood-stain on the library floor.

This certainly was very strange, as the door was always locked at night by Mr. Otis, and the windows kept closely barred.

The chameleon-like colour, also, of the stain excited a good deal of comment.

Some mornings it was a dull (almost Indian) red, then it would be vermilion, then a rich purple, and once when they came down for family prayers, according to the simple rites of the Free American Reformed Episcopalian Church, they found it a bright emerald-green.

These kaleidoscopic changes naturally amused the party very much, and bets on the subject were freely made every evening.

The only person who did not enter into the joke was little Virginia, who, for some unexplained reason, was always a good deal distressed at the sight of the blood-stain, and very nearly cried the morning it was emerald-green.

The second appearance of the ghost was on Sunday night.

Shortly after they had gone to bed they were suddenly alarmed by a fearful crash in the hall.

„Andererseits", fuhr Mr. Otis fort, „wenn er wirklich und durchaus den Rising Sun Lubricator nicht benutzen will, so werden wir ihm seine Ketten fortnehmen müssen; bei dem Lärm auf dem Korridor kann man ganz unmöglich schlafen."

Die Schlossbewohner blieben jedoch die ganze Woche hindurch ungestört, und das einzige, was ihre Aufmerksamkeit erregte, war die beständige Erneuerung des Blutflecks auf dem Boden der Bibliothek.

Das war jedenfalls sehr sonderbar, da die Tür und das Fenster des Nachts immer fest verschlossen und verriegelt waren.

Auch die wechselnde Farbe des Fleckes rief die verschiedensten Vermutungen hervor.

Denn zuweilen war er ganz mattrot (fast Indisch), dann wieder leuchtend, oder auch tiefpurpurn, und als einmal die Familie zum Gebet herunterkam (im Einklang mit dem einfachen Zeremonien der 'Free American Reformed Episcopalian Church'), fand sie ihn hell smaragdgrün!

Diese koloristischen Metamorphosen amüsierten natürlich die Gesellschaft sehr und jeden Abend wurden schon Wetten darüber geschlossen.

Die einzige, welche nicht auf diesen und keinen andern Scherz einging, war die kleine Virginia, die aus irgendeinem unaufgeklärten Grunde immer sehr betrübt beim Anblick des Blutflecks war und an dem Morgen, an dem er smaragdgrün leuchtete, bitterlich zu weinen anfing.

Das zweite Auftreten des Gespenstes war am Sonntagabend.

Kurz nachdem auch die männlichen Erwachsenen zu Bett gegangen waren, wurden sie plötzlich durch ein

Rushing down-stairs, they found that a large suit of old armour had become detached from its stand, and had fallen on the stone floor, while seated in a high-backed chair was the Canterville ghost, rubbing his knees with an expression of acute agony on his face.

The twins, having brought their pea-shooters with them, at once discharged two pellets on him, with that accuracy of aim which can only be attained by long and careful practice on a writing-master, while the United States Minister covered him with his revolver, and called upon him, in accordance with Californian etiquette, to hold up his hands!

The ghost started up with a wild shriek of rage, and swept through them like a mist, extinguishing Washington Otis's candle as he passed, and so leaving them all in total darkness.

On reaching the top of the staircase he recovered himself, and determined to give his celebrated peal of demoniac laughter. This he had on more than one occasion found extremely useful.

It was said to have turned Lord Raker's wig grey in a single night, and had certainly made three of Lady Canterville's French governesses give warning before their month was up.

He accordingly laughed his most horrible laugh, till the old vaulted roof rang and rang again, but hardly had the fearful echo died away when a door opened, and Mrs. Otis came out in a light blue dressing-gown.

furchtbares Getöse in der Eingangshalle aufgeschreckt.

Alle stürzten hinunter und fanden dort, dass eine alte Rüstung von ihrem Ständer auf den Steinboden gefallen war, während das Gespenst von Canterville in einem hochlehnigen Armstuhl saß und sich seine Knie mit einer Gebärde verzweifelten Schmerzes rieb.

Die Zwillinge hatten ihre Flitzbogen mitgebracht und schossen zweimal nach ihm mit einer Treffsicherheit, die sie sich durch lange sorgfältige Übungen nach ihrem Schreiblehrer erworben hatten. Der Gesandte der Vereinigten Staaten richtete unterdessen seinen Revolver auf den Geist und rief ihm nach kalifornischer Etikette zu: „Hände hoch!"

Der Geist fuhr mit einem wilden Wutgeheul in die Höhe und mitten durch die Familie hin wie ein Rauch, indem er noch Washingtons Kerzenlicht ausblies und sie alle in völliger Dunkelheit zurückließ.

Oben au der Treppe erholte sich das Gespenst wieder und beschloss, in sein berühmtes diabolisches Gelächter auszubrechen; das hatte sich ihm bei mehr als einer Gelegenheit schon nützlich erwiesen.

Es soll Lord Rakers Perücke in einer einzigen Nacht gebleicht haben und hat jedenfalls drei der französischen Gouvernanten von Lady Canterville so entsetzt, dass sie vor der Zeit und ohne Kündigung ihre Stellungen aufgaben.

So lachte er denn also jetzt dieses sein fürchterlichstes Lachen, bis das alte hochgewölbte Dach davon gellte; aber kaum war das letzte grausige Echo verhallt, da öffnete sich eine Tür, und Mrs. Otis kam heraus in einem hellblauen Morgenrock.

"I am afraid you are far from well," she said, "and have brought you a bottle of Doctor Dobell's tincture.

If it is indigestion, you will find it a most excellent remedy."

The ghost glared at her in fury, and began at once to make preparations for turning himself into a large black dog, an accomplishment for which he was justly renowned, and to which the family doctor always attributed the permanent idiocy of Lord Canterville's uncle, the Hon. Thomas Horton.

The sound of approaching footsteps, however, made him hesitate in his fell purpose, so he contented himself with becoming faintly phosphorescent, and vanished with a deep churchyard groan, just as the twins had come up to him.

On reaching his room he entirely broke down, and became a prey to the most violent agitation.

The vulgarity of the twins, and the gross materialism of Mrs. Otis, were naturally extremely annoying, but what really distressed him most was that he had been unable to wear the suit of mail.

He had hoped that even modern Americans would be thrilled by the sight of a Spectre in armour, if for no more sensible reason, at least out of respect for their natural poet Longfellow, over whose graceful and attractive poetry he himself had whiled away many a weary hour when the Cantervilles were up in town.

Besides it was his own suit.

„Ich fürchte, Ihnen ist nicht ganz wohl", sagte sie, „und deshalb bringe ich Ihnen hier eine Flasche von Dr. Dobells Tropfen.

Wenn es Verdauungsbeschwerden sind, so werden Sie finden, dass sie ein ganz vorzügliches Mittel sind."

Der Geist betrachtete sie zornesrot und wollte sich auf der Stelle in einen großen schwarzen Hund verwandeln — ein Kunststück, wodurch er mit Recht berühmt war und dem der Hausarzt die Geistesgestörtheit von Lord Cantervilles Onkel, Herrn Thomas Horton, zuschrieb.

Da hörte er aber Schritte und das ließ ihn von seinem grausen Vorhaben abstehen; er begnügte sich damit, phosphoreszierend zu werden, und verschwand mit einem dumpfen Kirchhofswimmern gerade in dem Moment, als die Zwillinge auf ihn zukamen.

Als der Geist sein Zimmer erreicht hatte, brach er völlig zusammen und verfiel in einen Zustand heftiger Gemütsbewegung.

Die Rohheit der Zwillinge und der krasse Materialismus von Mrs. Otis waren natürlich außerordentlich verstimmend; aber was ihn am meisten betrübte, war doch, dass er die alte Rüstung nicht mehr hatte tragen können.

Er hatte gehofft, dass sogar moderne Amerikaner erschüttert sein würden beim Anblick eines Gespenstes in Waffenrüstung, wenn auch aus keinem andern vernünftigen Grunde, so doch aus Achtung vor ihrem Nationalpoeten Longfellow, bei dessen graziöser und anziehender Poesie er selbst so manche Stunde hingebracht hatte, während die Cantervilles in London waren.

Und dabei war es noch seine eigene Rüstung!

He had worn it with great success at the Kenilworth tournament, and had been highly complimented on it by no less a person than the Virgin Queen herself.

Yet when he had put it on, he had been completely overpowered by the weight of the huge breastplate and steel casque, and had fallen heavily on the stone pavement, barking both his knees severely, and bruising the knuckles of his right hand.

For some days after this he was extremely ill, and hardly stirred out of his room at all, except to keep the blood-stain in proper repair.

However, by taking great care of himself, he recovered, and resolved to make a third attempt to frighten the United States Minister and his family.

He selected Friday, August 17th, for his appearance, and spent most of that day in looking over his wardrobe, ultimately deciding in favour of a large slouched hat with a red feather, a winding-sheet frilled at the wrists and neck, and a rusty dagger.

Towards evening a violent storm of rain came on, and the wind was so high that all the windows and doors in the old house shook and rattled.

In fact, it was just such weather as he loved.

His plan of action was this. He was to make his way quietly to Washington Otis's room, gibber at him from the foot of the bed, and stab himself three times in the throat to the sound of low music.

He bore Washington a special grudge, being quite aware that it was he who was in the habit of removing the famous

Er hatte sie mit großem Erfolg auf dem Turnier in Kenilworth getragen und darüber von niemand Geringerem als der jungfräulichen Königin selber viel Schmeichelhaftes gesagt bekommen.

Und als er die Rüstung heute anlegen wollte, hatte ihn das Gewicht des alten Panzers und Stahlhelmes so erdrückt, dass er darunter zu Boden gestürzt war, sich beide Knie heftig zerschlagen und die rechte Hand verstaucht hatte.

Mehrere Tage lang fühlte er sich nach diesem Vorfall ernstlich krank und verließ sein Zimmer nur, um den Blutfleck in Ordnung zu halten.

Da er sich sonst jedoch sehr schonte, erholte er sich bald wieder und beschloss, noch einen dritten Versuch zu machen, den Gesandten und seine Familie in Schrecken zu jagen.

Er wählte zu diesem seinem Auftreten Freitag, den 17. August, und beschäftigte sich den ganzen Tag damit, seine Kleidervorräte zu prüfen, bis er schließlich einen großen weichen Hut mit roter Feder, ein Laken mit Rüschen an Hals und Armen und einen rostigen Dolch wählte.

Gegen Abend kam ein heftiger Regenschauer und der Sturm rüttelte gewaltig an allen Türen und Fenstern des alten Hauses.

Das war gerade das Wetter, wie er es liebte.

Sein Plan war folgender: er wollte sich ganz leise zu Washingtons Zimmer schleichen, ihm vom Fußende des Bettes aus wirres Zeug vorschwatzen und sich dann beim Klang leiser geisterhafter Musik dreimal den Dolch ins Herz stoßen.

Er war auf Washington ganz besonders böse, weil er wusste, dass dieser es war, der immer wieder den Blutfleck mit

Canterville blood-stain by means of Pinkerton's Paragon Detergent.

Having reduced the reckless and foolhardy youth to a condition of abject terror, he was then to proceed to the room occupied by the United States Minister and his wife, and there to place a clammy hand on Mrs. Otis's forehead, while he hissed into her trembling husband's ear the awful secrets of the charnel-house.

With regard to little Virginia, he had not quite made up his mind.

She had never insulted him in any way, and was pretty and gentle.

A few hollow groans from the wardrobe, he thought, would be more than sufficient, or, if that failed to wake her, he might grabble at the counterpane with palsy-twitching fingers.

As for the twins, he was quite determined to teach them a lesson.

The first thing to be done was, of course, to sit upon their chests, so as to produce the stifling sensation of nightmare.

Then, as their beds were quite close to each other, to stand between them in the form of a green, icy-cold corpse, till they became paralyzed with fear, and finally, to throw off the winding-sheet, and crawl round the room, with white, bleached bones and one rolling eyeball, in the character of "Dumb Daniel, or the Suicide's Skeleton,"

a rôle in which he had on more than one occasion produced a great effect, and which he considered quite equal to his famous part of "Martin the Maniac, or the Masked Mystery."

Pinkertons Fleckenreiniger entfernte.

Wenn er dann den frivolen und tollkühnen Jüngling in den namenlosen Schrecken versetzt hatte, so wollte er sich zu dem Schlafzimmer von Herrn und Frau Otis begeben und dort eine eiskalte Hand Mrs. Otis auf die Stirn legen, während er ihrem zitternden Mann die entsetzlichen Geheimnisse des Beinhauses ins Ohr zischelte.

Was die kleine Virginia betraf, so war er über sie noch nicht ganz im reinen.

Sie hatte ihn nie in irgendeiner Weise beleidigt und war hübsch und sanft.

Einige tiefe Seufzer aus dem Kleiderschrank würden mehr als genug für sie sein, dachte er, und wenn sie davon noch nicht aufwachte, so könnte er ja mit zitternden Fingern an ihrem Betttuch zerren.

In Bezug auf die Zwillinge war er aber fest entschlossen, ihnen eine ordentliche Lektion zu erteilen.

Das erste war natürlich, dass er sich ihnen auf die Brust setzte, um das erstickende Gefühl eines Alpdrückens hervorzurufen.

Dann würde er, da ihre Betten dicht nebeneinander standen, in der Gestalt eines grünen, eiskalten Leichnams zwischen ihnen stehen, bis sie vor Schrecken gelähmt waren; und zum Schluss wollte er mit weißgebleichten Knochen und einem rollenden Augapfel ums Zimmer herumkriechen als ‚Stummer Daniel oder das Skelett des Selbstmörders'.

Diese Rolle hatte bei mehr als einer Gelegenheit den allergrößten Effekt gemacht und schien ihm so gut zu sein wie seine berühmte Darstellung des ‚Martin, des Verrückten, oder das verhüllte Geheimnis'.

At half-past ten he heard the family going to bed.

For some time he was disturbed by wild shrieks of laughter from the twins, who, with the light-hearted gaiety of schoolboys, were evidently amusing themselves before they retired to rest, but at a quarter-past eleven all was still, and, as midnight sounded, he sallied forth.

The owl beat against the window-panes, the raven croaked from the old yew-tree, and the wind wandered moaning round the house like a lost soul; but the Otis family slept unconscious of their doom, and high above the rain and storm he could hear the steady snoring of the Minister for the United States.

He stepped stealthily out of the wainscoting, with an evil smile on his cruel, wrinkled mouth, and the moon hid her face in a cloud as he stole past the great oriel window, where his own arms and those of his murdered wife were blazoned in azure and gold.

On and on he glided, like an evil shadow, the very darkness seeming to loathe him as he passed.

Once he thought he heard something call, and stopped; but it was only the baying of a dog from the Red Farm, and he went on, muttering strange sixteenth-century curses, and ever and anon brandishing the rusty dagger in the midnight air.

Finally he reached the corner of the passage that led to luckless Washington's room.

For a moment he paused there, the wind

Um halb elf Uhr hörte er die Familie zu Bette gehen.

Er wurde noch einige Zeit durch das Lachgebrüll der Zwillinge gestört, die mit der leichtfertigen Heiterkeit von Schuljungen sich augenscheinlich herrlich amüsierten, ehe sie zu Bett gingen; aber um ein Viertel zwölf Uhr war alles still; und als es Mitternacht schlug, machte er sich auf den Weg.

Die Eule schlug mit den Flügeln gegen die Fensterscheiben, der Rabe krächzte von dem alten Eichbaum und der Wind ächzte durch das Haus wie eine verlorene Seele; aber die Familie Otis schlief, unbekümmert um das nahende Verhängnis, und durch und trotz Regen und Sturm hörte man das regelmäßige Schnarchen des Gesandten der Union.

Da trat er heimlich aus der Vertäfelung hervor, mit einem bösen Lächeln um den grausamen, faltigen Mund, so dass sogar der Mond sein Gesicht verbarg, als er an dem hohen Fenster vorüberglitt, auf dem das Wappen des Gespenstes und das seiner ermordeten Frau in Gold und Hellblau gemalt waren.

Weiter und weiter glitt er, wie ein böser Schatten; die Dunkelheit selber schien sich vor ihm zu grausen, wie er vorbeihuschte.

Einmal kam es ihm vor, als hörte er jemand rufen; er stand still; aber es war nur das Bellen eines Hundes auf dem nahen Bauernhof, und so schlich er weiter, während er wunderliche Flüche aus dem sechzehnten Jahrhundert vor sich hin murmelte und dann und wann mit dem rostigen Dolch in der Luft herumstach.

Nun hatte er die Ecke des Korridors erreicht, der zu des unglücklichen Washington Zimmer führte.

Einen Augenblick blieb er da stehen,

blowing his long grey locks about his head, and twisting into grotesque and fantastic folds the nameless horror of the dead man's shroud.

Then the clock struck the quarter, and he felt the time was come.

He chuckled to himself, and turned the corner; but no sooner had he done so than, with a piteous wail of terror, he fell back, and hid his blanched face in his long, bony hands. Right in front of him was standing a horrible spectre, motionless as a carven image, and monstrous as a madman's dream!

Its head was bald and burnished; its face round, and fat, and white; and hideous laughter seemed to have writhed its features into an eternal grin.

From the eyes streamed rays of scarlet light, the mouth was a wide well of fire, and a hideous garment, like to his own, swathed with its silent snows the Titan form.

On its breast was a placard with strange writing in antique characters, some scroll of shame it seemed, some record of wild sins, some awful calendar of crime, and, with its right hand, it bore aloft a falchion of gleaming steel.

Never having seen a ghost before, he naturally was terribly frightened, and, after a second hasty glance at the awful phantom, he fled back to his room, tripping up in his long winding-sheet as he sped down the corridor, and finally dropping the rusty dagger into the Minister's jack-boots, where it was found in the morning by the butler.

und der Wind blies ihm seine langen grauen Locken um den Kopf und spielte ein phantastisches und groteskes Spiel mit den unheimlichen Falten des Leichentuchs.

Da schlug die Uhr ein Viertel und er fühlte, jetzt sei die Zeit gekommen.

Er kicherte vor sich hin und machte einen Schritt um die Ecke; aber kaum tat er das, da fuhr er mit einem jammervollen Schreckenslaut zurück und verbarg sein erblasstes Gesicht in den langen knochigen Händen: gerade vor ihm stand ein entsetzliches Gespenst, bewegungslos wie eine gemeißelte Statue und fürchterlich wie der Traum eines Wahnsinnigen!

Der Kopf war kahl und glänzend, das Gesicht rund und fett und weiß, und grässliches Lachen schien seine Züge in ein ewiges Grinsen verzerrt zu haben.

Aus den Augen kamen rote Lichtstrahlen, der Mund war eine weite Feuerhöhle, und ein scheußliches Gewand, seinem eigenen ähnlich, verhüllte mit seinem schneeigen Weiß die Gestalt des Riesen.

Auf seiner Brust war ein Plakat befestigt, mit einer sonderbaren Schrift in antiken Buchstaben — wohl irgendein Bericht wilder Missetaten, ein schmähliches Verzeichnis schauerlicher Verbrechen —, und in seiner rechten Hand hielt es einen Stichel aus blitzendem Stahl.

Da der Geist noch nie in seinem Leben ein Gespenst gesehen hatte, so war er natürlich furchtbar erschrocken; und nachdem er noch einen zweiten hastigen Blick auf die entsetzliche Erscheinung geworfen hatte, floh er zu seinem Zimmer zurück, stolperte über sein langes Laken, als er den Korridor hinunterraste, und ließ schließlich noch seinen Dolch in die hohen Jagdstiefel

Once in the privacy of his own apartment, he flung himself down on a small pallet-bed, and hid his face under the clothes.

After a time, however, the brave old Canterville spirit asserted itself, and he determined to go and speak to the other ghost as soon as it was daylight.

Accordingly, just as the dawn was touching the hills with silver, he returned towards the spot where he had first laid eyes on the grisly phantom, feeling that, after all, two ghosts were better than one, and that, by the aid of his new friend, he might safely grapple with the twins.

On reaching the spot, however, a terrible sight met his gaze.

Something had evidently happened to the spectre, for the light had entirely faded from its hollow eyes, the gleaming falchion had fallen from its hand, and it was leaning up against the wall in a strained and uncomfortable attitude.

He rushed forward and seized it in his arms, when, to his horror, the head slipped off and rolled on the floor, the body assumed a recumbent posture, and he found himself clasping a white dimity bed-curtain, with a sweeping-brush, a kitchen cleaver, and a hollow turnip lying at his feet!

Unable to understand this curious transformation, he clutched the placard with feverish haste, and there, in the grey morning light, he read these fearful words:

YE OTIS GHOSTE
Ye Onlie True and Originale Spook,

des Gesandten fallen, wo ihn der Kammerdiener am nächsten Morgen fand.

In seinem Zimmer angekommen, warf er sich auf das schmale Feldbett und verbarg sein Gesicht unter der Decke.

Nach einer Weile jedoch rührte sich der tapfere alte Cantervillecharakter doch wieder, und der Geist beschloss, sobald der Tag graute, zu dem andern Geist zu gehen und ihn anzureden.

Kaum begann es zu dämmern, da machte er sich auf und ging zur Stelle, wo seine Augen zuerst das grässliche Phantom erblickt hatten; denn er fühlte, es sei doch schließlich angenehmer, zwei Gespenster zusammen zu sein als eines allein, und dass er mit Hilfe dieses neuen Freundes erfolgreich gegen die Zwillinge zu Felde ziehen könne.

Als er jedoch an die Stelle kam, bot sich ihm ein fürchterlicher Anblick.

Dem Gespenst war jedenfalls ein Unglück passiert, denn in seinen hohlen Augen war das Licht erloschen, die glänzende Keule war seiner Hand entfallen, und es selber lehnte in einer höchst unbequemen gezwungenen Stellung an der Wand.

Er stürzte vorwärts und zog es am Arme, da fiel zu seinem Entsetzen der Kopf ab, rollte auf den Boden, der Körper fiel in sich zusammen, und er hielt in seinen Händen eine weiße Bettgardine mit einem Besenstiel und einem Küchenbeil, während zu seinen Füßen ein hohler Kürbis lag!

Unfähig, diese wunderbare Veränderung zu begreifen, packte er mit wilder Hast das Plakat, und da las er im grauen Licht des Morgens die fürchterlichen Worte:

Das Otis - Gespenst.
Der einzig wahre und originale Spuk.

Beware of Ye Imitationes.

All others are counterfeite.

The whole thing flashed across him.

He had been tricked, foiled, and out-witted!

The old Canterville look came into his eyes; he ground his toothless gums together; and, raising his withered hands high above his head, swore according to the picturesque phraseology of the antique school, that, when Chanticleer had sounded twice his merry horn, deeds of blood would be wrought, and murder walk abroad with silent feet.

Hardly had he finished this awful oath when, from the red-tiled roof of a distant homestead, a cock crew.

He laughed a long, low, bitter laugh, and waited.

Hour after hour he waited, but the cock, for some strange reason, did not crow again.

Finally, at half-past seven, the arrival of the housemaids made him give up his fearful vigil, and he stalked back to his room, thinking of his vain oath and baffled purpose.

There he consulted several books of ancient chivalry, of which he was exceedingly fond, and found that, on every occasion on which this oath had been used, Chanticleer had always crowed a second time.

"Perdition seize the naughty fowl," he muttered, "I have seen the day when, with my stout spear, I would have run him through the gorge, and made him crow for me an 'twere in death!"

Vor Nachahmung wird gewarnt.

Alle anderen sind unecht.

Jetzt war ihm alles klar.

Man hatte ihn zum besten gehalten und er war hineingefallen!

Der alte wilde Cantervilleblick kam in seine Augen; er kniff den zahnlosen Mund zusammen, und indem er seine knochigen Hände hoch in die Höhe warf, schwor er in der pittoresken Phraseologie des alten Stiles: wenn Chanticleer zum zweiten Mal in sein lustiges Horn stieße, würden entsetzliche Bluttaten geschehen, und Mord würde auf leisen Sohlen durchs Haus schleichen.

Kaum hatte er diesen furchtbaren Schwur zu Ende geschworen, als vom roten Ziegeldach eines Bauernhofes der Hahn krähte.

Das Gespenst lachte ein langes, dumpfes, bitteres Lachen und wartete.

Stunde auf Stunde wartete er, aber der Hahn krähte aus irgendeinem Grunde nicht wieder.

Endlich ließ ihn um halb acht das Kommen der Hausmädchen seine grausige Nachtwache aufgeben und er ging zu seinem Zimmer, in tiefen Gedanken über seinen vergeblichen Schwur und sein vereiteltes Vorhaben.

Er schlug in verschiedenen alten Ritterbüchern nach, was er außerordentlich liebte, und fand, dass noch jedes Mal, wo dieser Schwur getan, Chanticleer ein zweites Mal gekräht hatte.

„Zum Teufel mit dem faulen Hahn", brummte er, „hätte ich doch den Tag erlebt, wo ich mit meinem sicheren Speer ihm durch die Gurgel gefahren wäre, und da würde er, wenn auch schon im Sterben, für mich zweimal haben krähen müssen!"

He then retired to a comfortable lead coffin, and stayed there till evening.

Hierauf legte er sich in einem kostbaren ehernen Sarg zur Ruhe und blieb da bis zum späten Abend.

Chapter 4

The next day the ghost was very weak and tired.

Am folgenden Tage war der Geist sehr schwach und müde.

The terrible excitement of the last four weeks was beginning to have its effect. His nerves were completely shattered, and he started at the slightest noise.

Die furchtbaren Aufregungen der letzten vier Wochen fingen an, ihn anzugreifen, seine Nerven waren völlig kaputt, und beim geringsten Geräusch fuhr er erschreckt in die Höhe.

For five days he kept his room, and at last made up his mind to give up the point of the blood-stain on the library floor.

Fünf Tage lang blieb er still auf seinem Zimmer und fand sich darein, die ewige Sorge um den Blutfleck in der Bibliothek aufzugeben.

If the Otis family did not want it, they clearly did not deserve it.

Wenn die Familie Otis den Fleck nicht zu haben wünschte, so war sie ihn auch nicht wert.

They were evidently people on a low, material plane of existence, and quite incapable of appreciating the symbolic value of sensuous phenomena.

Das waren überhaupt augenscheinlich Leute von ganz niederer Bildung und völlig unfähig, den symbolischen Wert eines Hausgespenstes zu würdigen.

The question of phantasmic apparitions, and the development of astral bodies, was of course quite a different matter, and really not under his control.

Die Frage nach überirdischen Erscheinungen und der Entwicklung der Himmelskörper war natürlich eine ganz andere Sache, aber die ging ihn nichts an.

It was his solemn duty to appear in the corridor once a week, and to gibber from the large oriel window on the first and third Wednesdays in every month, and he did not see how he could honourably escape from his obligations.

Seine heilige Pflicht war es, einmal in der Woche auf dem Korridor zu spuken und jeden 1. und 3. Mittwoch im Monat von dem großen bunten Glasfenster aus wirres Zeug zu schwatzen: von diesen beiden Verpflichtungen konnte er sich ehrenhalber nicht freimachen.

It is quite true that his life had been very evil, but, upon the other hand, he was most conscientious in all things connected with the supernatural.

Gewiss war ja sein Leben ein äußerst böses gewesen, aber anderseits musste man zugeben, dass er in allen Dingen, die mit dem Übernatürlichen zusammenhingen, außerordentlich

For the next three Saturdays, accordingly, he traversed the corridor as usual between midnight and three o'clock, taking every possible precaution against being either heard or seen.

He removed his boots, trod as lightly as possible on the old worm-eaten boards, wore a large black velvet cloak, and was careful to use the Rising Sun Lubricator for oiling his chains.

I am bound to acknowledge that it was with a good deal of difficulty that he brought himself to adopt this last mode of protection.

However, one night, while the family were at dinner, he slipped into Mr. Otis's bedroom and carried off the bottle.

He felt a little humiliated at first, but afterwards was sensible enough to see that there was a great deal to be said for the invention, and, to a certain degree, it served his purpose.

Still in spite of everything he was not left unmolested.

Strings were continually being stretched across the corridor, over which he tripped in the dark, and on one occasion, while dressed for the part of "Black Isaac, or the Huntsman of Hogley Woods," he met with a severe fall, through treading on a butter-slide, which the twins had constructed from the entrance of the Tapestry Chamber to the top of the oak staircase.

This last insult so enraged him, that he resolved to make one final effort to assert his dignity and social position, and determined to visit the insolent

gewissenhaft war.

Demgemäß wanderte er also an den folgenden drei Samstagen wie gewöhnlich zwischen zwölf und drei Uhr die Korridore auf und ab, gab aber schrecklich darauf acht, dass er weder gehört noch gesehen wurde.

Er zog die Stiefel aus und trat so leise wie möglich auf die alten wurmstichigen Böden; er trug einen weiten schwarzen Samtmantel und gebrauchte den Rising Sun Lubricator gewissenhaft, um seine Ketten damit zu schmieren.

Dieses letzte Vorsichtsmittel benutzte er, wie ich zugeben muss, erst nach vielen Schwierigkeiten.

Eines Abends jedoch, während die Familie gerade beim Essen saß, schlich er sich in Mr. Otis' Schlafzimmer und holte sich die Flasche.

Zuerst fühlte er sich wohl ein wenig gedemütigt, aber schließlich war er doch vernünftig genug, einzusehen, dass diese Erfindung etwas für sich hatte, und jedenfalls diente sie bis zu einem gewissen Grade seinen Zwecken.

Aber trotz alledem ließ man ihn noch immer nicht ganz unbelästigt.

Beständig waren Stricke über den Korridor gespannt, über die er im Dunkeln natürlich fiel; und eines Abends, als er gerade als ‚Schwarzer Isaak oder der Jäger vom Hogleywald' angezogen war, stürzte er plötzlich heftig zu Boden, weil er auf einer Schleifbahn von Butter, welche die Zwillinge vom Tapetenzimmer bis zur Eichentreppe hergerichtet hatten, ausgeglitten war.

Diese letzte Beleidigung brachte ihn so in Wut, dass er beschloss, nur noch eine letzte Anstrengung zu machen, um seine Würde und seine gesellschaftliche

young Etonians the next night in his celebrated character of "Reckless Rupert, or the Headless Earl."

He had not appeared in this disguise for more than seventy years; in fact, not since he had so frightened pretty Lady Barbara Modish by means of it, that she suddenly broke off her engagement with the present Lord Canterville's grandfather, and ran away to Gretna Green with handsome Jack Castletown, declaring that nothing in the world would induce her to marry into a family that allowed such a horrible phantom to walk up and down the terrace at twilight.

Poor Jack was afterwards shot in a duel by Lord Canterville on Wandsworth Common, and Lady Barbara died of a broken heart at Tunbridge Wells before the year was out, so, in every way, it had been a great success.

It was, however an extremely difficult "make-up," if I may use such a theatrical expression in connection with one of the greatest mysteries of the supernatural, or, to employ a more scientific term, the higher-natural world, and it took him fully three hours to make his preparations.

At last everything was ready, and he was very pleased with his appearance.

The big leather riding-boots that went with the dress were just a little too large for him, and he could only find one of the two horse-pistols, but, on the whole, he was quite satisfied, and at a quarter-past one he glided out of the wainscoting and crept down the

Stellung zu sichern, und dies sollte damit geschehen, dass er den frechen jungen Etonschülern die nächste Nacht in seiner berühmten Rolle als ‚Kühner Ruprecht oder der Graf ohne Kopf' erscheinen wollte.

Seit mehr als siebzig Jahren war er nicht in dieser Rolle aufgetreten, seit er damals die hübsche Lady Barbara Modish so damit erschreckt hatte, dass sie plötzlich ihre Verlobung mit dem Großvater des jetzigen Lord Canterville auflöste und statt dessen mit dem schönen Jack Castletown nach Gretna Green floh, indem sie erklärte, um keinen Preis der Welt in eine Familie hineinheiraten zu wollen, die einem abscheulichen Gespenst erlaube, in der Dämmerung auf der Terrasse spazieren zu gehen.

Der arme Jack wurde später vom Lord Canterville im Duell am Wandsworthgehölz erschossen und Lady Barbara starb, noch ehe das Jahr vergangen war, in Tunbridge Wells an gebrochenem Herzen; so war also damals sein Erscheinen von größtem Erfolge gewesen.

Aber es war mit dieser Rolle sehr viel Mühe verbunden, wenn ich so sagen darf in Hinsicht auf eines der größten Geheimnisse des Übernatürlichen, und er brauchte volle drei Stunden zu den Vorbereitungen.

Endlich war alles fertig und er war sehr zufrieden mit seinem Aussehen.

Die großen ledernen Reitstiefel, die zum Kostüme gehörten, waren ihm zwar ein bisschen zu weit, und er konnte nur eine der beiden großen Pistolen finden; aber im ganzen genommen war er doch angetan von sich, und um ein Viertel nach ein Uhr glitt er ans der

corridor.

On reaching the room occupied by the twins, which I should mention was called the Blue Bed Chamber, on account of the colour of its hangings, he found the door just ajar.

Wishing to make an effective entrance, he flung it wide open, when a heavy jug of water fell right down on him, wetting him to the skin, and just missing his left shoulder by a couple of inches.

At the same moment he heard stifled shrieks of laughter proceeding from the four-post bed.

The shock to his nervous system was so great that he fled back to his room as hard as he could go, and the next day he was laid up with a severe cold.

The only thing that at all consoled him in the whole affair was the fact that he had not brought his head with him, for, had he done so, the consequences might have been very serious.

He now gave up all hope of ever frightening this rude American family, and contented himself, as a rule, with creeping about the passages in list slippers, with a thick red muffler round his throat for fear of draughts, and a small arquebuse, in case he should be attacked by the twins.

The final blow he received occurred on the 19th of September.

He had gone down-stairs to the great entrance-hall, feeling sure that there, at any rate, he would be quite unmolested, and was amusing himself by making satirical remarks on the large Saroni photographs of the United States Minister and his wife which had now taken the place of the Canterville family

Wandtäfelung hervor und schlich den Korridor hinab.

Als er das Zimmer der Zwillinge erreicht hatte, das, wie ich erwähnen muss, wegen seiner Vorhänge auch das blaue Schlafzimmer genannt wurde, fand er die Tür nur angelehnt.

Da er nun einen effektvollen Eintritt wünschte, so stieß er sie weit auf — schwupp! da fiel ein schwerer Wasserkrug gerade auf ihn herunter und durchnässte ihn bis auf die Haut.

Im gleichen Augenblick hörte er unterdrücktes Gelächter vom Bett herkommen.

Der Schock, den sein Nervensystem erlitt, war so stark, dass er, so schnell er nur konnte, zu seinem Zimmer lief; den nächsten Tag lag er an einer heftigen Erkältung fest im Bett.

Sein einziger Trost bei der Sache war, dass er seinen Kopf nicht bei sich gehabt hatte, denn wäre dies der Fall gewesen, so hätten die Folgen doch sehr ernste sein können.

Jetzt gab er alle Hoffnung auf, diese ordinären Amerikaner überhaupt noch zu erschrecken, und begnügte sich in der Regel damit, in Pantoffeln über den Korridor zu schleichen, mit einem dicken rotwollenen Tuch um den Hals, aus Angst vor Zugluft, und einer kleinen Armbrust, im Fall ihn die Zwillinge angreifen sollten.

Aber der Hauptschlag, der gegen ihn geführt wurde, geschah am 19. September.

Er war in die große Eingangshalle hingegangen, da er sich dort noch am wenigsten behelligt wusste, und unterhielt sich damit, spöttische Bemerkungen über die lebensgroßen Platinphotographien des Gesandten und seiner Frau zu machen, welche jetzt an Stelle der Canterville-Ahnenbilder

pictures.

He was simply but neatly clad in a long shroud, spotted with churchyard mould, had tied up his jaw with a strip of yellow linen, and carried a small lantern and a sexton's spade.

In fact, he was dressed for the character of "Jonas the Graveless, or the Corpse-Snatcher of Chertsey Barn," one of his most remarkable impersonations, and one which the Cantervilles had every reason to remember, as it was the real origin of their quarrel with their neighbour, Lord Rufford.

It was about a quarter-past two o'clock in the morning, and, as far as he could ascertain, no one was stirring.

As he was strolling towards the library, however, to see if there were any traces left of the blood-stain, suddenly there leaped out on him from a dark corner two figures, who waved their arms wildly above their heads, and shrieked out "BOO!" in his ear.

Seized with a panic, which, under the circumstances, was only natural, he rushed for the staircase, but found Washington Otis waiting for him there with the big garden-syringe, and being thus hemmed in by his enemies on every side, and driven almost to bay, he vanished into the great iron stove, which, fortunately for him, was not lit, and had to make his way home through the flues and chimneys, arriving at his own room in a terrible state of dirt, disorder, and despair.

After this he was not seen again on any nocturnal expedition.

hingen.

Er war einfach, aber ordentlich gekleidet, und zwar in ein langes Laken, das da und dort bräunliche Flecken von Kirchhofserde aufwies, hatte seine untere Kinnlade mit einem Stück gelber Leinwand hochgebunden und trug eine kleine Laterne und den Spaten eines Totengräbers.

Eigentlich war es das Kostüm von ,Jonas, dem Grablosen, oder der Leichenräuber von Chertsey Barn', eine seiner hervorragendsten Rollen, welche die Cantervilles allen Grund hatten zu kennen, weil durch sie der ewige Streit mit ihrem Nachbarn Lord Rufford verursacht worden war.

Es war so gegen Viertel nach zwei Uhr morgens und allem Anschein nach rührte sich nichts.

Als er jedoch langsam zu der Bibliothek schlenderte, um doch mal wieder nach den etwaigen Spuren des Blutflecks zu sehen, da sprangen aus einer dunklen Ecke plötzlich zwei Gestalten hervor, welche ihre Arme wild emporwarfen und ihm „Buh!" in die Ohren brüllten.

Von panischem Schrecken ergriffen, der unter solchen Umständen nur selbstverständlich erscheinen muss, raste er zu der Treppe, wo aber schon Washington mit der großen Gartenspritze auf ihn wartete; da er sich nun von seinen Feinden so umzingelt und fast zur Verzweiflung getrieben sah, verschwand er schleunigst in den großen eisernen Ofen, der zu seinem Glück nicht angesteckt war, und musste nun auf einem höchst beschwerlichen Weg durch Ofenrohre und Kamine zu seinem Zimmer zurück, wo er völlig erschöpft, beschmutzt und verzweifelt ankam.

Nach diesem Erlebnis wurde er nie mehr auf einer solchen nächtlichen

The twins lay in wait for him on several occasions, and strewed the passages with nutshells every night to the great annoyance of their parents and the servants, but it was of no avail.

It was quite evident that his feelings were so wounded that he would not appear.

Mr. Otis consequently resumed his great work on the history of the Democratic Party, on which he had been engaged for some years;

Mrs. Otis organized a wonderful clambake, which amazed the whole county;

the boys took to lacrosse euchre, poker, and other American national games, and Virginia rode about the lanes on her pony, accompanied by the young Duke of Cheshire, who had come to spend the last week of his holidays at Canterville Chase.

It was generally assumed that the ghost had gone away, and, in fact, Mr. Otis wrote a letter to that effect to Lord Canterville, who, in reply, expressed his great pleasure at the news, and sent his best congratulations to the Minister's worthy wife.

The Otises, however, were deceived, for the ghost was still in the house, and though now almost an invalid, was by no means ready to let matters rest,

particularly as he heard that among the guests was the young Duke of Cheshire, whose grand-uncle, Lord Francis Stilton, had once bet a hundred guineas with Colonel Carbury that he would

Expedition getroffen.

Die Zwillinge warteten bei den verschiedensten Gelegenheiten auf sein Erscheinen und streuten jede Nacht den Korridor ganz voll Nussschalen, zum großen Ärger ihrer Eltern und der Dienerschaft, aber es war alles vergebens.

Augenscheinlich waren die Gefühle des armen Gespenstes derart verletzt, dass es sich nicht wieder zeigen wollte.

In der Folge nahm dann Mr. Otis sein großes Werk über die Geschichte der demokratischen Partei wieder auf, das ihn schon seit Jahren beschäftigte;

Mrs. Otis organisierte ein wunderbares Preiskuchenbacken, das die ganze Grafschaft aufregte;

die Jungen gaben sich dem Vergnügen von Lacrosse, Euchre, Poker und andern amerikanischen Nationalspielen hin, und Virginia ritt auf ihrem hübschen Pony im Park spazieren, begleitet von dem jungen Herzog von Cheshire, der die letzten Wochen der großen Ferien auf Schloss Canterville verleben durfte.

Man nahm allgemein an, dass der Geist das Schloss verlassen habe, ja Mr. Otis schrieb sogar einen Brief in diesem Sinn an Lord Canterville, der in Erwiderung desselben seine große Freude über diese Nachricht aussprach und sich der werten Frau Gemahlin ausdrücklich empfehlen ließ.

Die Familie Otis hatte sich aber getäuscht, denn der Geist war noch im Hause, und obgleich fast ein Schwerkranker, so war er doch keinesfalls entschlossen, die Sache ruhen zu lassen,

besonders als er hörte, dass unter den Gästen auch der junge Herzog von Cheshire sich befinde, dessen Großonkel Lord Francis Stilton einst um 1000 Guineen mit Oberst Carbury

play dice with the Canterville ghost, and was found the next morning lying on the floor of the card-room in such a helpless paralytic state that,

though he lived on to a great age, he was never able to say anything again but "Double Sixes."

The story was well known at the time, though, of course, out of respect to the feelings of the two noble families, every attempt was made to hush it up, and a full account of all the circumstances connected with it will be found in the third volume of Lord Tattle's 'Recollections of the Prince Regent and his Friends'.

The ghost, then, was naturally very anxious to show that he had not lost his influence over the Stiltons, with whom, indeed, he was distantly connected, his own first cousin having been married _en secondes noces_ to the Sieur de Bulkeley, from whom, as every one knows, the Dukes of Cheshire are lineally descended.

Accordingly, he made arrangements for appearing to Virginia's little lover in his celebrated impersonation of "The Vampire Monk, or the Bloodless Benedictine,"

a performance so horrible that when old Lady Startup saw it, which she did on one fatal New Year's Eve, in the year 1764, she went off into the most piercing shrieks, which culminated in violent apoplexy, and died in three days, after disinheriting the Cantervilles, who were her nearest relations, and leaving all her money to her London apothecary.

At the last moment, however, his terror of the twins prevented his leaving his

---

gewettet hatte, dass er mit dem Geist Würfel spielen wollte, und der am nächsten Morgen im Spielzimmer auf dem Boden liegend, in einem Zustand hilfloser Lähmung gefunden wurde.

Obgleich er noch ein hohes Alter erreichte, so war er niemals wieder imstande gewesen, etwas anderes als ‚Zwei Atout' zu sagen.

Die Geschichte war seinerzeit allgemein bekannt, obgleich natürlich aus Rücksicht auf die beiden vornehmen Familien die größten Anstrengungen gemacht wurden, sie zu vertuschen; aber der ausführliche Bericht mit allen näheren Umständen ist in dem dritten Band von Lord Tattles Erinnerungen an den Prinz-Regenten und seine Freunde zu finden.

Der Geist war natürlich sehr besorgt, zu zeigen, dass er seine Macht über die Stiltons noch nicht verloren hätte, mit denen er ja noch dazu entfernt verwandt war, da seine rechte Cousine in zweiter Ehe mit dem Sir de Bulkeley vermählt war, von dem, wie allgemein bekannt, die Herzöge von Cheshire abstammen.

Demgemäß traf er Vorkehrungen, Virginias kleinem Liebhaber in seiner berühmten Rolle als,Vampirmönch oder der blutlose Benediktiner' zu erscheinen.

Dies war eine so fürchterliche Aufführung, dass Lady Startup an jenem verhängnisvollen Neujahrsabend 1764 vor Schreck von einem Gehirnschlag getroffen wurde, an dem sie nach drei Tagen starb, nachdem sie noch schnell die Cantervilles, ihre nächsten Verwandten, enterbt und ihren ganzen Besitz ihrem Londoner Apotheker vermacht hatte.

Im letzten Moment aber verhinderte den Geist die Angst vor den Zwillingen, sein

room, and the little Duke slept in peace under the great feathered canopy in the Royal Bedchamber, and dreamed of Virginia.

Zimmer zu verlassen, und der kleine Herzog schlief friedlich in seinem hohen Himmelbett im königlichen Schlafzimmer und träumte von Virginia.

Chapter 5

A few days after this, Virginia and her curly-haired cavalier went out riding on Brockley meadows, where she tore her habit so badly in getting through a hedge that, on their return home, she made up her mind to go up by the back staircase so as not to be seen.

Wenige Tage später ritten Virginia und ihr goldlockiger junger Ritter über die Brockleywiesen spazieren, wo sie beim Springen über eine Hecke ihr Reitkleid derart zerriss, dass sie, zu Hause angekommen, vorzog, die Hintertreppe hinaufzugehen, um nicht gesehen zu werden.

As she was running past the Tapestry Chamber, the door of which happened to be open, she fancied she saw some one inside, and thinking it was her mother's maid, who sometimes used to bring her work there, looked in to ask her to mend her habit.

Als sie an dem alten Gobelinzimmer vorüberkam, dessen Tür zufällig halb offen stand, meinte sie jemanden drinnen zu sehen, und da sie ihrer Mama Kammermädchen darin vermutete, die dort zuweilen arbeitete, so ging sie hinein, um gleich ihr Kleid ausbessern zu lassen.

To her immense surprise, however, it was the Canterville Ghost himself!

Zu ihrer ungeheuren Überraschung war es jedoch das Gespenst von Canterville selber!

He was sitting by the window, watching the ruined gold of the yellowing trees fly through the air, and the red leaves dancing madly down the long avenue.

Es saß am Fenster und beobachtete, wie das matte Gold des vergilbten Laubes durch die Luft flog und die roten Blätter einen wilden Reigen in der langen Allee tanzten.

His head was leaning on his hand, and his whole attitude was one of extreme depression.

Es hatte den Kopf in die Hand gestützt und seine ganze Haltung drückte tiefe Niedergeschlagenheit aus.

Indeed, so forlorn, and so much out of repair did he look, that little Virginia, whose first idea had been to run away and lock herself in her room, was filled with pity, and determined to try and comfort him.

Ja, so verlassen und verfallen sah es aus, dass die kleine Virginia, deren erster Gedanke gewesen war, zu fliehen und sich in ihr Zimmer einzuschließen, von Mitleid erfüllt sich entschloss zu bleiben, um das arme Gespenst zu trösten.

So light was her footfall, and so deep his melancholy, that he was not aware of her presence till she spoke to him.

"I am so sorry for you," she said, "but my brothers are going back to Eton to-morrow, and then, if you behave yourself, no one will annoy you."

"It is absurd asking me to behave myself," he answered, looking round in astonishment at the pretty little girl who had ventured to address him, "quite absurd.

I must rattle my chains, and groan through keyholes, and walk about at night, if that is what you mean.

It is my only reason for existing."

"It is no reason at all for existing, and you know you have been very wicked.

Mrs. Umney told us, the first day we arrived here, that you had killed your wife."

"Well, I quite admit it," said the Ghost, petulantly, "but it was a purely family matter, and concerned no one else."

"It is very wrong to kill any one," said Virginia, who at times had a sweet puritan gravity, caught from some old New England ancestor.

"Oh, I hate the cheap severity of abstract ethics!

My wife was very plain, never had my ruffs properly starched, and knew nothing about cookery.

Why, there was a buck I had shot in Hogley Woods, a magnificent pricket,

Ihr Schritt war so leicht und seine Melancholie so tief, dass es ihre Gegenwart erst bemerkte, als sie zu ihm sprach.

„Sie tun mir so leid", sagte sie, „aber morgen müssen meine Brüder nach Eton zurück, und wenn Sie sich dann wie ein gebildeter Mensch befragen wollen, so wird Sie niemand mehr ärgern."

„Das ist ein einfältiges und ganz unsinniges Verlangen einem Geist gegenüber", antwortete er, indem er erstaunt das hübsche kleine Mädchen ansah, das ihn anzureden wagte.

„Ich muss mit meinen Ketten rasseln und durch Schlüssellöcher stöhnen und des Nachts herumwandeln, wenn es das ist, was Sie meinen.

Das ist ja mein einziger Lebenszweck."

„Das ist überhaupt kein Lebenszweck, und Sie wissen sehr gut, dass Sie ein böser, schlechter Mensch gewesen sind.

Mrs. Umney hat uns am ersten Tag unseres Hierseins gesagt, dass Sie Ihre Frau getötet haben."

„Nun ja, das gebe ich zu", sagte das Gespenst geärgert, „aber das war doch eine reine Familienangelegenheit und ging niemand anderen etwas an."

„Es ist sehr unrecht, jemand umzubringen", sagte Virginia, die zeitweise einen ungemein lieblichen puritanischen Ernst besaß, mit dem sie von irgendeinem Vorfahren aus Neu-England belastet war.

„O, wie ich die billige Strenge abstrakter Moral hasse!

Meine Frau war sehr hässlich, hat mir niemals die Manschetten ordentlich stärken lassen und verstand nichts vom Kochen.

Denken Sie nur, einst hatte ich einen Kapitalbock im Hogleywald

and do you know how she had it sent to table?

However, it is no matter now, for it is all over, and I don't think it was very nice of her brothers to starve me to death, though I did kill her."

"Starve you to death? Oh, Mr. Ghost--I mean Sir Simon, are you hungry?

I have a sandwich in my case. Would you like it?"

"No, thank you, I never eat anything now; but it is very kind of you, all the same, and you are much nicer than the rest of your horrid, rude, vulgar, dishonest family."

"Stop!"

cried Virginia, stamping her foot, "it is you who are rude, and horrid, and vulgar, and as for dishonesty, you know you stole the paints out of my box to try and furbish up that ridiculous blood-stain in the library.

First you took all my reds, including the vermilion, and I couldn't do any more sunsets, then you took the emerald-green and the chrome-yellow, and finally I had nothing left but indigo and Chinese white, and could only do moonlight scenes, which are always depressing to look at, and not at all easy to paint.

I never told on you, though I was very much annoyed, and it was most ridiculous, the whole thing; for who ever heard of emerald-green blood?"

"Well, really," said the Ghost, rather

geschossen, und wissen Sie, wie sie ihn auf den Tisch brachte?

Aber das ist ja jetzt ganz gleichgültig, denn es ist lange her, und ich kann nicht finden, dass es nett von ihren Brüdern war, mich zu Tode hungern zu lassen, bloß weil ich sie getötet hatte."

„Sie zu Tode hungern? O, lieber Herr Geist, ich meine Sir Simon, sind Sie hungrig?

Ich habe ein Butterbrot bei mir, möchten Sie das haben?"

„Nein, ich danke Ihnen sehr, ich nehme jetzt nie mehr etwas zu mir; aber trotzdem ist es sehr freundlich von Ihnen, und Sie sind überhaupt viel netter als alle anderen Ihrer abscheulich groben, vulgären, unehrlichen Familie."

„Schweigen Sie!"

rief Virginia und stampfte mit dem Fuß, „Sie sind es, der grob, abscheulich und gewöhnlich ist, und was die Unehrlichkeit betrifft, so wissen Sie sehr wohl, dass Sie mir alle Farben aus meinem Malkasten gestohlen haben, um den lächerlichen Blutfleck in der Bibliothek stets frisch zu machen!

Erst nahmen Sie alle die roten, sogar Vermillon, und ich konnte gar keine Sonnenuntergänge mehr malen, dann nahmen Sie Smaragdgrün und Chromgelb, und schließlich blieb mir nichts mehr als Indigo und Chinesisch-weiß, da konnte ich nur noch Mondschein-Landschaften malen, die immer solchen melancholischen Eindruck machen und gar nicht leicht zu malen sind.

Ich habe Sie nie verraten, obgleich ich sehr ärgerlich war, und die ganze Sache war ja überhaupt lächerlich; denn wer hat je im Leben von grünen Blutflecken gehört?"

„Ja, aber was sollte ich tun", sagte der

meekly, "what was I to do? It is a very difficult thing to get real blood nowadays, and, as your brother began it all with his Paragon Detergent, I certainly saw no reason why I should not have your paints.

As for colour, that is always a matter of taste: the Cantervilles have blue blood, for instance, the very bluest in England; but I know you Americans don't care for things of this kind."

"You know nothing about it, and the best thing you can do is to emigrate and improve your mind.

My father will be only too happy to give you a free passage, and though there is a heavy duty on spirits of every kind, there will be no difficulty about the Custom House, as the officers are all Democrats.

Once in New York, you are sure to be a great success.

I know lots of people there who would give a hundred thousand dollars to have a grandfather, and much more than that to have a family ghost."

"I don't think I should like America."

"I suppose because we have no ruins and no curiosities," said Virginia, satirically.

"No ruins!

no curiosities!"

answered the Ghost; "you have your navy and your manners." "Good evening; I will go and ask papa to get the twins an extra week's holiday."

"Please don't go, Miss Virginia," he cried; "I am so lonely and so unhappy,

Geist kleinlaut; „heutzutage ist es schwer, wirkliches Blut zu bekommen, und als Ihr Bruder nun mit seinem Fleckenreiniger anfing, da sah ich wirklich nicht ein, warum ich nicht Ihre Farben nehmen sollte.

Was nun die besondere Färbung betrifft, so ist das lediglich Geschmackssache; die Cantervilles z. B. haben blaues Blut, das allerblaueste in England: aber ich weiß, Ihr Amerikaner macht Euch aus dergleichen nichts."

„Darüber wissen Sie gar nichts, und das beste wäre, Sie wanderten aus und vervollkommneten drüben Ihre Bildung.

Mein Vater wird nur zu glücklich sein, Ihnen freie Überfahrt zu verschaffen, und wenn auch ein hoher Zoll auf Geistiges jeder Art liegt, so wird es doch auf dem Zollamt keine Schwierigkeiten geben, denn die Beamten sind alle Demokraten.

Wenn Sie erst mal in New York sind, so garantiere ich Ihnen einen großen Erfolg.

Ich kenne eine Menge Leute, die tausend Dollars dafür geben würden, einen Großvater zu haben, und noch unendlich viel mehr für ein Familiengespenst."

„Ich glaube, mir würde Amerika nicht gefallen."

„Wahrscheinlich weil wir keine Ruinen und Altertümer haben", sagte Virginia spöttisch.

„Keine Ruinen?

Keine Altertümer?"

erwiderte der Geist, „Sie haben doch Ihre Marine und Ihre Umgangsformen!" „Guten Abend; ich gehe jetzt und will Papa bitten, den Zwillingen noch extra acht Tage länger Ferien zu geben."

„Bitte, gehen Sie nicht, Miss Virginia", rief das Gespenst; „ich bin so einsam

and I really don't know what to do.

I want to go to sleep and I cannot."

"That's quite absurd!
You have merely to go to bed and blow out the candle.

It is very difficult sometimes to keep awake, especially at church, but there is no difficulty at all about sleeping.

Why, even babies know how to do that, and they are not very clever."

"I have not slept for three hundred years," he said sadly, and Virginia's beautiful blue eyes opened in wonder; "for three hundred years I have not slept, and I am so tired."

Virginia grew quite grave, and her little lips trembled like rose-leaves.

She came towards him, and kneeling down at his side, looked up into his old withered face.

"Poor, poor Ghost," she murmured; "have you no place where you can sleep?"

"Far away beyond the pine-woods," he answered, in a low, dreamy voice, "there is a little garden.

There the grass grows long and deep, there are the great white stars of the hemlock flower, there the nightingale sings all night long.

All night long he sings, and the cold crystal moon looks down, and the yew-tree spreads out its giant arms over the sleepers."

Virginia's eyes grew dim with tears, and she hid her face in her hands.

und unglücklich und weiß nicht mehr, was ich tun soll.

Ich möchte nur schlafen und kann es doch nicht."

„Das ist töricht!

Sie brauchen doch nur zu Bett zu gehen und das Licht auszublasen.

Manchmal ist es so schwer, wach zu bleiben, besonders in der Kirche; aber beim Einschlafen gibt es doch gar keine Schwierigkeiten.

Sogar die kleinen Kinder können das und sind doch gar nicht klug."

„Seit dreihundert Jahren habe ich nicht mehr geschlafen", sagte das Gespenst traurig, und Virginias schöne blaue Augen öffneten sich weit in grenzenlosem Erstaunen, „seit dreihundert Jahren habe ich nicht mehr geschlafen, und ich bin so müde."

Virginia wurde auf einmal ganz ernst, und ihre kleinen Lippen zitterten wie Rosenblätter.

Sie trat näher zu ihm, kniete sich an seine Seite und sah zu seinem alten gefurchten Gesicht auf.

„Armer, armer Geist", sprach sie leise, „haben Sie denn kein Fleckchen, wo Sie mal schlafen können?"

„Weit hinter jenen Wäldern liegt ein kleiner Garten", sagte der Geist mit verträumter ferner Stimme.

„Da wächst langes Gras, da blühen die großen weißen Sterne des Schierlings, und die Nachtigallen singen die ganze Nacht hindurch.

Die ganze lange Nacht singen sie und der kalte, kristallene Mond schaut nieder, und die Trauerweide breitet ihre Riesenarme über die Schläfer aus."

Virginias Augen füllten sich mit Tränen, und sie verbarg das Gesicht in den Händen.

"You mean the Garden of Death," she whispered.

"Yes, death.

Death must be so beautiful.

To lie in the soft brown earth, with the grasses waving above one's head, and listen to silence.

To have no yesterday, and no to-morrow.

To forget time, to forget life, to be at peace.

You can help me.

You can open for me the portals of death's house, for love is always with you, and love is stronger than death is."

Virginia trembled, a cold shudder ran through her, and for a few moments there was silence.

She felt as if she was in a terrible dream.

Then the ghost spoke again, and his voice sounded like the sighing of the wind.

"Have you ever read the old prophecy on the library window?"

"Oh, often," cried the little girl, looking up; "I know it quite well.

It is painted in curious black letters, and is difficult to read. There are only six lines:

"'When a golden girl can win
Prayer from out the lips of sin,
When the barren almond bears,
And a little child gives away its tears,
Then shall all the house be still
And peace come to Canterville.'

„Sie meinen den Garten des Todes“, flüsterte sie.

„Ja, Tod.

Der Tod muss so schön sein.

In der weichen braunen Erde zu liegen, während das lange Gras über einem hin und her schwankt, und der Stille zu lauschen.

Kein Gestern, kein Morgen haben.

Die Zeit und das Leben vergessen, im Frieden sein.

Sie können mir helfen.

Sie können mir die Tore des Todes öffnen, denn auf Ihrer Seite ist stets die Liebe, und die Liebe ist stärker als der Tod.“

Virginia zitterte, und ein kalter Schauer durchlief sie, und einige Minuten lang war es still.

Es schien ihr wie ein angstvoller Traum.

Dann sprach der Geist wieder und seine Stimme klang wie das Seufzen des Windes.

„Haben Sie je die alte Prophezeiung an dem Fenster in der Bibliothek gelesen?“

„O, wie oft“, rief das junge Mädchen aufblickend, „ich kenne sie sehr gut.

Sie ist mit verschnörkelten schwarzen Buchstaben geschrieben und schwer zu lesen; es sind nur sechs Zeilen:

Wenn ein goldenes Mädchen es dahin bringt,
dass es sündige Lippen zum Beten zwingt,
Wenn die dürre Mandel unter den Blüten sich senkt
ein unschuldiges Kind seine Tränen verschenkt,
Dann wird dies Haus wieder ruhig und still,
und der Friede kehrt ein auf Schloss

"But I don't know what they mean."

"They mean," he said, sadly, "that you must weep with me for my sins, because I have no tears, and pray with me for my soul, because I have no faith, and then, if you have always been sweet, and good, and gentle, the angel of death will have mercy on me.

You will see fearful shapes in darkness, and wicked voices will whisper in your ear, but they will not harm you, for against the purity of a little child the powers of Hell cannot prevail."

Virginia made no answer, and the ghost wrung his hands in wild despair as he looked down at her bowed golden head.

Suddenly she stood up, very pale, and with a strange light in her eyes.

"I am not afraid," she said firmly, "and I will ask the angel to have mercy on you."

He rose from his seat with a faint cry of joy, and taking her hand bent over it with old-fashioned grace and kissed it.

His fingers were as cold as ice, and his lips burned like fire, but Virginia did not falter, as he led her across the dusky room.

On the faded green tapestry were broidered little huntsmen. They blew their tasselled horns and with their tiny hands waved to her to go back.

"Go back! little Virginia," they cried, "go back!"

but the ghost clutched her hand more tightly, and she shut her eyes against them.

Horrible animals with lizard tails and goggle eyes blinked at her from the carven chimneypiece, and murmured,

Canterville.

Aber ich weiß nicht, was das heißen soll."

„Das heißt: dass Sie für mich über meine Sünden weinen müssen, da ich keine Tränen habe, und für mich, für meine Seele beten müssen, da ich keinen Glauben habe, und dann, wenn Sie immer gut und sanft gewesen sind, dann wird der Engel des Todes Erbarmen mit mir haben.

Sie werden entsetzliche Gestalten im Dunkeln sehen, Schauriges wird Ihr Ohr vernehmen, aber es wird Ihnen kein Leid geschehen, denn gegen die Reinheit eines Kindes sind die Gewalten der Hölle ohne Macht."

Virginia antwortete nicht, und der Geist rang verzweifelt die Hände, während er auf ihr gesenktes Köpfchen herabsah.

Plötzlich erhob sie sich, ganz blass, aber ihre Augen leuchteten.

„Ich fürchte mich nicht", sagte sie bestimmt, „ich will den Engel bitten, Erbarmen mit Ihnen zu haben."

Mit einem leisen Freudenausruf stand der Geist auf, ergriff mit altmodischer Galanterie ihre Hand und küsste sie.

Seine Finger waren kalt wie Eis und seine Lippen brannten wie Feuer, aber Virginia zauderte nicht, als er sie durch das dämmerdunkle Zimmer führte.

In den verblassten grünen Gobelin waren kleine Jäger gewirkt, die bliesen auf ihren Hörnern und winkten ihr mit den winzigen Minden, umzukehren.

,Kehre um, kleine Virginia,' riefen sie, ,kehre um!'

Aber der Geist fasste ihre Hand fester und sie schloss die Augen.

Gräuliche Tiere mit Eidechsenschwänzen und feurigen Augen sahen sie vom Kaminsims an

"Beware! little Virginia, beware! we may never see you again," but the Ghost glided on more swiftly, and Virginia did not listen.

When they reached the end of the room he stopped, and muttered some words she could not understand.

She opened her eyes, and saw the wall slowly fading away like a mist, and a great black cavern in front of her.

A bitter cold wind swept round them, and she felt something pulling at her dress.

"Quick, quick," cried the Ghost, "or it will be too late," and in a moment the wainscoting had closed behind them, and the Tapestry Chamber was empty.

Chapter 6

About ten minutes later, the bell rang for tea, and, as Virginia did not come down, Mrs. Otis sent up one of the footmen to tell her.

After a little time he returned and said that he could not find Miss Virginia anywhere.

As she was in the habit of going out to the garden every evening to get flowers for the dinner-table, Mrs. Otis was not at all alarmed at first, but when six o'clock struck, and Virginia did not appear, she became really agitated, and sent the boys out to look for her, while she herself and Mr. Otis searched every room in the house.

At half-past six the boys came back and

und grinsten: ‚Nimm dich in acht, Virginia, nimm dich in acht! Vielleicht sieht man dich nie wieder!' Aber der Geist ging noch schneller voran und Virginia hörte nicht auf die Stimmen.

Am Ende des Zimmers hielt das Gespenst an und murmelte einige Worte, die sie nicht verstand.

Sie schlug die Augen auf und sah die Wand vor sich verschwinden wie im Nebel, und eine große schwarze Höhle tat sich auf.

Es wurde ihr eisig kalt und sie fühlte etwas an ihrem Kleide zerren.

„Schnell, schnell", rief der Geist, „sonst ist es zu spät", und schon hatte sich die Wand hinter ihnen wieder geschlossen, und das Gobelinzimmer war leer.

Ungefähr zehn Minuten später tönte der Gong zum Tee und da Virginia nicht herunterkam, schickte Mrs. Otis einen Diener hinauf, sie zu rufen.

Nach kurzer Zeit kam er wieder und sagte, dass er Miss Virginia nirgends habe finden können.

Da sie um diese Zeit gewöhnlich in den Garten ging, um Blumen für den Mittagstisch zu pflücken, so war Mrs. Otis zuerst gar nicht weiter besorgt; aber als es sechs Uhr schlug und Virginia immer noch nicht da war, wurde sie doch unruhig und schickte die Jungen aus, sie zu suchen, während sie und Mr. Otis das ganze Haus abgingen.

Um halb sieben kamen die Jungen

said that they could find no trace of their sister anywhere.

They were all now in the greatest state of excitement, and did not know what to do, when Mr. Otis suddenly remembered that, some few days before, he had given a band of gipsies permission to camp in the park.

He accordingly at once set off for Blackfell Hollow, where he knew they were, accompanied by his eldest son and two of the farm-servants.

The little Duke of Cheshire, who was perfectly frantic with anxiety, begged hard to be allowed to go too, but Mr. Otis would not allow him, as he was afraid there might be a scuffle.

On arriving at the spot, however, he found that the gipsies had gone, and it was evident that their departure had been rather sudden, as the fire was still burning, and some plates were lying on the grass.

Having sent off Washington and the two men to scour the district, he ran home, and despatched telegrams to all the police inspectors in the county, telling them to look out for a little girl who had been kidnapped by tramps or gipsies.

He then ordered his horse to be brought round, and, after insisting on his wife and the three boys sitting down to dinner, rode off down the Ascot road with a groom.

He had hardly, however, gone a couple of miles, when he heard somebody galloping after him, and, looking round, saw the little Duke coming up on his pony, with his face very flushed, and no hat.

wieder und berichteten, sie hätten nirgends auch nur eine Spur von ihrer Schwester entdecken können.

Jetzt waren alle auf das äußerste beunruhigt und wussten nicht mehr, was sie tun sollten, als Mr. Otis sich plötzlich darauf besann, dass er vor einigen Tagen einer Zigeunerbande erlaubt habe, im Park zu übernachten.

So machte er sich denn sofort auf nach Blackfell Hollow, wo sich die Bande, wie er wusste, jetzt aufhielt, und sein ältester Sohn und zwei Bauernburschen begleiteten ihn.

Der kleine Herzog von Cheshire, der vor Angst ganz außer sich war, bat inständigst, sich anschließen zu dürfen; aber Mr. Otis wollte es ihm nicht erlauben, da er fürchtete, der junge Herr würde in seiner Aufregung nur stören.

Als sie jedoch an die gesuchte Stelle kamen, waren die Zigeuner fort, und zwar war ihr Abschied augenscheinlich ein sehr rascher gewesen, wie das noch brennende Feuer und einige auf dem Grase liegende Teller anzeigten.

Nachdem er Washington weiter auf die Suche geschickt hatte, eilte Mr. Otis heim und sandte Depeschen an alle Polizeiposten der Grafschaft, in denen er sie ersuchte, nach einem kleinen Mädchen zu forschen, das von Landstreichern oder Zigeunern entführt worden sei.

Dann ließ er sein Pferd satteln, und nachdem er darauf bestanden hatte, dass seine Frau und die beiden Jungen sich zu Tisch setzten, ritt er mit einem Knecht nach Ascot.

Aber kaum hatte er ein paar Meilen zurückgelegt, als er jemand hinter sich her galoppieren hörte; es war der junge Herzog, der auf seinem Pony mit erhitztem Gesicht und ohne Hut hinter ihm herkam.

"I'm awfully sorry, Mr. Otis," gasped out the boy, "but I can't eat any dinner as long as Virginia is lost.

Please don't be angry with me; if you had let us be engaged last year, there would never have been all this trouble.

You won't send me back, will you?

I can't go! I won't go!"

The Minister could not help smiling at the handsome young scapegrace, and was a good deal touched at his devotion to Virginia, so leaning down from his horse, he patted him kindly on the shoulders, and said, "Well, Cecil, if you won't go back, I suppose you must come with me, but I must get you a hat at Ascot."

"Oh, bother my hat!

I want Virginia!"

cried the little Duke, laughing, and they galloped on to the railway station.

There Mr. Otis inquired of the station-master if any one answering to the description of Virginia had been seen on the platform, but could get no news of her.

The station-master, however, wired up and down the line, and assured him that a strict watch would be kept for her, and, after having bought a hat for the little Duke from a linen-draper, who was just putting up his shutters, Mr. Otis rode off to Bexley, a village about four miles away, which he was told was a well-known haunt of the gipsies, as there was a large common next to it.

„Ich bitte um Verzeihung, Mr. Otis", sagte er atemlos, „aber ich kann nicht zu Abend essen, solange Virginia nicht gefunden ist.

Bitte, seien Sie mir nicht böse; wenn Sie voriges Jahr Ihre Einwilligung zu unserer Verlobung gegeben hätten, so würde all diese Sorge uns erspart geblieben sein.

Sie schicken mich nicht zurück, nicht wahr?

Ich kann nicht gehen und ich werde nicht gehen!

Der Gesandte musste lächeln über den hübschen Jungen und war wirklich gerührt über seine Liebe zu Virginia; so lehnte er sich denn zu ihm hinüber, klopfte ihm freundlich auf die Schulter und sagte: „Nun gut, Cecil, wenn Sie nicht umkehren wollen, so müssen Sie mit mir kommen, aber dann muss ich Ihnen in Ascot erst einen Hut kaufen."

„Ach, zum Teufel mit meinem Hut!

Ich will Virginia wiederhaben!",

rief der kleine Herzog lachend, und sie ritten weiter zu der Bahnstation.

Dort erkundigte sich Mr. Otis bei dem Bahnhofsvorsteher, ob nicht eine junge Dame auf dem Perron gesehen worden sei, auf welche die Beschreibung von Virginia passe; aber er konnte nichts über sie erfahren.

Der Bahnhofsvorsteher telegraphierte auf der Strecke hinauf und hinunter und versicherte Mr. Otis, dass man auf das gewissenhafteste recherchieren werde; und nachdem Mr. Otis noch bei einem Schnittwarenhändler, der eben seinen Laden schließen wollte, dem jungen Herzog einen Hut gekauft hatte, ritten sie nach Bexley weiter, einem Dorf, das ungefähr vier Meilen entfernt lag und bei dem die Zigeuner besonders gern ihr Lager aufschlugen, weil es bei einer

Here they roused up the rural policeman, but could get no information from him, and, after riding all over the common, they turned their horses' heads homewards, and reached the Chase about eleven o'clock, dead-tired and almost heart-broken.

They found Washington and the twins waiting for them at the gate-house with lanterns, as the avenue was very dark.

Not the slightest trace of Virginia had been discovered.

The gipsies had been caught on Brockley meadows, but she was not with them, and they had explained their sudden departure by saying that they had mistaken the date of Chorton Fair, and had gone off in a hurry for fear they should be late.

Indeed, they had been quite distressed at hearing of Virginia's disappearance, as they were very grateful to Mr. Otis for having allowed them to camp in his park, and four of their number had stayed behind to help in the search.

The carp-pond had been dragged, and the whole Chase thoroughly gone over, but without any result.

It was evident that, for that night at any rate, Virginia was lost to them; and it was in a state of the deepest depression that Mr. Otis and the boys walked up to the house, the groom following behind with the two horses and the pony.

In the hall they found a group of frightened servants, and lying on a sofa in the library was poor Mrs. Otis, almost out of her mind with terror and anxiety, and having her forehead bathed with

großen Wiese lag.

Hier weckten sie den Gendarmen, konnten aber nichts von ihm in Erfahrung bringen; und nachdem sie die ganze Gegend abgesucht hatten, mussten sie sich schließlich unverrichteter Dinge auf den Heimweg machen und erreichten todmüde und gebrochenen Herzens um elf Uhr wieder das Schloss.

Sie fanden Washington und die Zwillinge am Tor, wo sie mit Laternen gewartet hatten, weil die Allee so dunkel war.

Nicht die geringste Spur von Virginia hatte man bisher entdecken können.

Man hatte die Zigeuner auf den Wiesen von Brockley eingeholt, aber sie war nicht bei ihnen, und die Zigeuner hatten ihre plötzliche Abreise damit erklärt, dass sie eiligst auf den Jahrmarkt von Chorton hätten müssen, um dort nicht zu spät anzukommen.

Es hatte ihnen wirklich herzlich leid getan, von Virginias Verschwinden zu hören, und da sie Mr. Otis dankbar waren, weil er ihnen den Aufenthalt in seinem Park gestattet hatte, so waren vier von der Bande mit zurückgekommen, um sich an der Suche zu beteiligen.

Man ließ den Karpfenteich ab und durchsuchte jeden Winkel im Schloss — alles ohne Erfolg.

Es war kein Zweifel, Virginia war, wenigstens für diese Nacht, verloren. In tiefster Niedergeschlagenheit kehrten Mr. Otis und die Jungen in das Haus zurück, während der Knecht mit den beiden Pferden und dein Pony folgte.

In der Halle standen alle Dienstboten aufgeregt beieinander und auf einem Sofa in der Bibliothek lag die arme Mrs. Otis, die vor Schrecken und Angst fast den Verstand verloren hatte und der die

eau de cologne by the old housekeeper.

Mr. Otis at once insisted on her having something to eat, and ordered up supper for the whole party.

It was a melancholy meal, as hardly any one spoke, and even the twins were awestruck and subdued, as they were very fond of their sister.

When they had finished, Mr. Otis, in spite of the entreaties of the little Duke, ordered them all to bed, saying that nothing more could be done that night, and that he would telegraph in the morning to Scotland Yard for some detectives to be sent down immediately.

Just as they were passing out of the dining-room, midnight began to boom from the clock tower, and when the last stroke sounded they heard a crash and a sudden shrill cry; a dreadful peal of thunder shook the house, a strain of unearthly music floated through the air, a panel at the top of the staircase flew back with a loud noise, and out on the landing, looking very pale and white, with a little casket in her hand, stepped Virginia.

In a moment they had all rushed up to her.

Mrs. Otis clasped her passionately in her arms, the Duke smothered her with violent kisses, and the twins executed a wild war-dance round the group.

"Good heavens!

child, where have you been?"

said Mr. Otis, rather angrily, thinking that she had been playing some foolish trick on them.

"Cecil and I have been riding all over the country looking for you, and your

gute alte Haushälterin die Stirn mit Eau de Cologne wusch.

Mr. Otis bestand darauf, dass sie etwas esse, und bestellte das Diner für die ganze Familie.

Es war eine trübselige Mahlzeit, wo kaum einer ein Wort sprach; sogar die Zwillinge waren vor Schrecken stumm, denn sie liebten ihre Schwester sehr.

Als man fertig war, schickte Mr. Otis trotz der dringenden Bitten des jungen Herzogs alle zu Bett, indem er erklärte, dass man jetzt in der Nacht ja doch nichts mehr tun könne, und am nächsten Morgen wolle er sofort nach Scotland Yard telegraphieren, dass man ihnen mehrere Detektive schicken solle.

Gerade als man den Speisesaal verließ, schlug die große Turmuhr Mitternacht, und als der letzte Schlag verklungen war, hörte man plötzlich ein furchtbares Gepolter und einen durchdringenden Schrei; ein wilder Donner erschütterte das Haus in seinem Grunde, ein Strom von überirdischer Musik durchzog die Luft, die Wandtäfelung oben an der Treppe flog mit tosendem Lärm zur Seite, und in der Öffnung stand, blass und weiß, mit einer kleinen Schatulle in der Hand — Virginia!

Im Nu waren alle zu ihr hinaufgestürmt.

Mrs. Otis presste sie leidenschaftlich in ihre Arme, der Herzog erstickte sie fast mit seinen Küssen, und die Zwillinge vollführten einen wilden Indianertanz um die Gruppe herum.

„Mein Gott!

Kind, wo bist du nur gewesen?"

rief Mr. Otis fast etwas ärgerlich, da er glaubte, sie habe sich einen törichten Scherz mit ihnen erlaubt.

„Cecil und ich sind meilenweit über Land geritten, dich zu suchen, und deine

mother has been frightened to death. You must never play these practical jokes any more."

"Except on the Ghost! except on the Ghost!"

shrieked the twins, as they capered about.

"My own darling, thank God you are found; you must never leave my side again," murmured Mrs. Otis, as she kissed the trembling child, and smoothed the tangled gold of her hair.

"Papa," said Virginia, quietly, "I have been with the Ghost.

He is dead, and you must come and see him.

He had been very wicked, but he was really sorry for all that he had done, and he gave me this box of beautiful jewels before he died."

The whole family gazed at her in mute amazement, but she was quite grave and serious; and, turning round, she led them through the opening in the wainscoting down a narrow secret corridor, Washington following with a lighted candle, which he had caught up from the table.

Finally, they came to a great oak door, studded with rusty nails.

When Virginia touched it, it swung back on its heavy hinges, and they found themselves in a little low room, with a vaulted ceiling, and one tiny grated window.

Imbedded in the wall was a huge iron ring, and chained to it was a gaunt skeleton, that was stretched out at full length on the stone floor, and seemed to be trying to grasp with its long fleshless fingers an old-fashioned trencher and

Mutter hat sich zu Tode geängstigt. Du musst nie wieder solche dummen Streiche machen."

„Nur das Gespenst darfst du foppen, nur das Gespenst!"

schrien die Zwillinge und sprangen umher wie verrückt.

„Mein Liebling, Gott sei Dank, dass wir dich wiederhaben, du darfst nie wieder von meiner Seite", sagte Mrs. Otis zärtlich, während sie die zitternde Virginia küsste und ihr die langen zerzausten Locken glatt strich.

„Papa", sagte Virginia ruhig, „ich war bei dem Gespenst.

Es ist tot und du musst kommen, es zu sehen.

Es ist in seinem Leben ein schlechter Mensch gewesen, aber es hat alle seine Sünden bereut, und ehe es starb, gab es mir diese Schatulle mit sehr kostbaren Juwelen."

Die ganze Familie starrte sie lautlos verwundert an, aber sie sprach in vollem Ernst, wandte sich um und führte sie durch die Öffnung in der Wandtäfelung einen engen geheimen Korridor entlang; Washington folgte mit einem Licht, das er vom Tisch genommen hatte.

Endlich gelangten sie zu einer schweren eichenen Tür, die ganz mit rostigen Nägeln beschlagen war.

Als Virginia sie berührte, flog sie in ihren schweren Angeln zurück, und man befand sich in einem kleinen niedrigen Zimmer mit gewölbter Decke und einem vergitterten Fenster;

ein schwerer eiserner Ring war in die Wand eingelassen, und daran angekettet lag ein riesiges Skelett, das der Länge nach auf dem steinernen Boden ausgestreckt war und mit seinen langen fleischlosen Fingern nach einem

ewer, that were placed just out of its reach.

The jug had evidently been once filled with water, as it was covered inside with green mould.

There was nothing on the trencher but a pile of dust.

Virginia knelt down beside the skeleton, and, folding her little hands together, began to pray silently, while the rest of the party looked on in wonder at the terrible tragedy whose secret was now disclosed to them.

"Hallo!" suddenly exclaimed one of the twins, who had been looking out of the window to try and discover in what wing of the house the room was situated.

"Hallo!

the old withered almond-tree has blossomed.

I can see the flowers quite plainly in the moonlight."

"God has forgiven him," said Virginia, gravely, as she rose to her feet, and a beautiful light seemed to illumine her face.

"What an angel you are!"

cried the young Duke, and he put his arm round her neck, and kissed her.

altmodischen Krug und Teller zu greifen versuchte, die man aber gerade so weit gestellt hatte, dass die Hand sie nicht erreichen konnte.

Der Krug war wohl einmal mit Wasser gefüllt gewesen, denn innen war er ganz mit grünem Schimmel überzogen.

Auf dem Zinnteller lag nur ein Häufchen Staub.

Virginia kniete neben dem Skelett nieder, faltete ihre kleinen Hände und betete still, während die übrigen mit Staunen die grausige Tragödie betrachteten, deren Geheimnis ihnen nun enthüllt war.

„Schaut doch!", rief plötzlich einer der Zwillinge, der aus dem Fenster gesehen hatte, um sich über die Lage des Zimmers zu orientieren.

„Schaut doch!

Der alte verdorrte Mandelbaum blüht ja!

Ich kann die Blüten ganz deutlich im Mondlicht sehen."

„Gott hat ihm vergeben!" sagte Virginia ernst, als sie sich erhob, und ihr Gesicht strahlte in unschuldiger Freude.

„Du bist ein Engel!",

rief der junge Herzog, schloss sie in seine Arme und küsste sie.

Chapter 7

Four days after these curious incidents, a funeral started from Canterville Chase at about eleven o'clock at night.

The hearse was drawn by eight black horses, each of which carried on its head a great tuft of nodding ostrich-plumes, and the leaden coffin was covered by a rich purple pall, on which was embroidered in gold the Canterville coat-of-arms.

By the side of the hearse and the coaches walked the servants with lighted torches, and the whole procession was wonderfully impressive. Lord Canterville was the chief mourner, having come up specially from Wales to attend the funeral, and sat in the first carriage along with little Virginia.

Then came the United States Minister and his wife, then Washington and the three boys, and in the last carriage was Mrs. Umney.

It was generally felt that, as she had been frightened by the ghost for more than fifty years of her life, she had a right to see the last of him.

A deep grave had been dug in the corner of the churchyard, just under the old yew-tree, and the service was read in the most impressive manner by the Rev. Augustus Dampier.

When the ceremony was over, the servants, according to an old custom observed in the Canterville family, extinguished their torches, and, as the

Vier Tage nach diesen höchst wunderbaren Ereignissen verließ ein Trauerzug nachts um elf Uhr Schloss Canterville.

Den Leichenwagen zogen acht schwarze Pferde, von denen jedes einen großen Panaché von nickenden Straußenfedern auf dem Kopfe trug, und der bleierne Sarg war mit einer kostbaren purpurnen Decke verhangen, auf welcher das Wappen derer von Canterville in Gold gestickt war.

Neben dem Wagen her schritten die Diener mit brennenden Fackeln und der ganze Zug machte einen äußerst feierlichen Eindruck. Lord Canterville als der Hauptleidtragende war zu diesem Begräbnis extra von Wales gekommen und saß im ersten Wagen neben der kleinen Virginia.

Dann kam der Gesandte der Vereinigten Staaten und seine Gemahlin, danach Washington und die zwei Jungen, und im letzten Wagen saß Mrs. Umney, die alte Wirtschafterin, ganz allein.

Man hatte die Empfindung gehabt, dass sie, nachdem sie mehr als fünfzig Jahre ihres Lebens durch das Gespenst erschreckt worden war, nun auch ein Recht hätte, seiner Beerdigung beizuwohnen.

In der Ecke des Friedhofes war ein tiefes Grab gegraben, gerade unter der Trauerweide, und Hochwürden Augustus Dampier hielt eine höchst eindrucksvolle Grabrede.

Als die Zeremonie vorüber war, löschten die Diener, einer alten Familiensitte der Canterville gemäß, ihre Fackeln aus, und während der Sarg

coffin was being lowered into the grave, Virginia stepped forward, and laid on it a large cross made of white and pink almond-blossoms.

As she did so, the moon came out from behind a cloud, and flooded with its silent silver the little churchyard, and from a distant copse a nightingale began to sing.

She thought of the ghost's description of the Garden of Death, her eyes became dim with tears, and she hardly spoke a word during the drive home.

The next morning, before Lord Canterville went up to town, Mr. Otis had an interview with him on the subject of the jewels the ghost had given to Virginia.

They were perfectly magnificent, especially a certain ruby necklace with old Venetian setting, which was really a superb specimen of sixteenth-century work, and their value was so great that Mr. Otis felt considerable scruples about allowing his daughter to accept them.

"My lord," he said, "I know that in this country mortmain is held to apply to trinkets as well as to land, and it is quite clear to me that these jewels are, or should be, heirlooms in your family.

I must beg you, accordingly, to take them to London with you, and to regard them simply as a portion of your property which has been restored to you under certain strange conditions.

As for my daughter, she is merely a child, and has as yet, I am glad to say, but little interest in such appurtenances of idle luxury.

I am also informed by Mrs. Otis, who, I

in das Grab hinuntergelassen wurde, trat Virginia vor und legte ein großes Kreuz aus weißen und rosafarbenen Mandelblüten darauf nieder.

Inzwischen kam der Mond hinter einer Wolke hervor und übersilberte den kleinen Friedhof, und im Gebüsch flötete eine Nachtigall.

Virginia dachte an des Gespenstes Beschreibung vom Garten des Todes, ihre Augen füllten sich mit Tränen, und sie sprach auf der Rückfahrt nicht ein Wort.

Am nächsten Morgen hatte Mr. Otis mit Lord Canterville vor dessen Rückkehr nach London eine Unterredung wegen der Juwelen, welche das Gespenst Virginia gegeben hatte.

Sie waren von ganz hervorragender Schönheit, besonders ein Halsschmuck von Rubinen in altvenezianischer Fassung, ein Meisterwerk der Kunst des sechzehnten Jahrhunderts, und so wertvoll, dass Mr. Otis zögerte, seiner Tochter zu erlauben, sie anzunehmen.

„Mylord", sagte er, „ich weiß sehr wohl, dass sich in diesem Lande die Erbfolge ebenso-wohl auf den Familienschmuck wie auf den Grundbesitz erstreckt, und ich bin dessen ganz sicher, dass diese Juwelen ein Erbstück Ihrer Familie sind oder doch sein sollten.

Ich muss Sie demgemäß bitten, sie mit nach London zu nehmen und sie einfach als Teil Ihres Eigentums zu betrachten, der unter allerdings höchst wunderbaren Umständen wieder in Ihren Besitz zurückgelangt ist.

Was meine Tochter betrifft, so ist diese ja noch ein Kind und hat, wie ich mich freue sagen zu können, nur wenig Interesse an solchen Luxusgegenständen.

Mrs. Otis, die, wie man wohl sagen

may say, is no mean authority upon Art,--having had the privilege of spending several winters in Boston when she was a girl,--that these gems are of great monetary worth, and if offered for sale would fetch a tall price.

Under these circumstances, Lord Canterville, I feel sure that you will recognize how impossible it would be for me to allow them to remain in the possession of any member of my family; and, indeed, all such vain gauds and toys, however suitable or necessary to the dignity of the British aristocracy, would be completely out of place among those who have been brought up on the severe, and I believe immortal, principles of Republican simplicity.

Perhaps I should mention that Virginia is very anxious that you should allow her to retain the box, as a memento of your unfortunate but misguided ancestor.

As it is extremely old, and consequently a good deal out of repair, you may perhaps think fit to comply with her request.

For my own part, I confess I am a good deal surprised to find a child of mine expressing sympathy with mediævalism in any form, and can only account for it by the fact that Virginia was born in one of your London suburbs shortly after Mrs. Otis had returned from a trip to Athens."

Lord Canterville listened very gravely to the worthy Minister's speech, pulling

kann, eine Autorität in Kunstsachen ist — da sie den großen Vorzug genossen hat, als junges Mädchen mehrere Winter in Boston zu verleben —, Mrs. Otis sagte mir, dass diese Juwelen einen sehr bedeutenden Wert repräsentieren und sich ganz vorzüglich verkaufen würden.

Unter diesen Umständen bin ich überzeugt, Lord Canterville, dass Sie einsehen werden, wie unmöglich es für mich ist, einem Mitglied meiner Familie zu erlauben, in dem Besitz der Juwelen zu bleiben, und endlich ist dieser eitle Putz und Tand und dieses glänzende Spielzeug, so passend und notwendig es auch zur Würde der britischen Aristokratie zu gehören scheint, doch unter jenen niemals recht am Platze, die in den strengen und, wie ich bestimmt glaube, unsterblichen Grundsätzen republikanischer Einfachheit erzogen sind.

Vielleicht sollte ich noch erwähnen, dass Virginia sehr gern die Schatulle selbst behalten möchte, als Erinnerung an Ihren unglücklichen, irregeleiteten Vorfahren.

Da selbe sehr alt und in einem Zustande großer Reparaturbedürftigkeit zu sein scheint, so werden Sie es vielleicht angemessen finden, der Bitte meiner Kleinen zu willfahren.

Ich für meinen Teil muss allerdings gestehen, dass ich außerordentlich erstaunt bin, eins von meinen Kindern Sympathie mit dem Mittelalter in irgendeiner Gestalt empfinden zu sehen, und ich kann mir das nicht anders als dadurch erklären, dass Virginia in einer Ihrer Londoner Vorstädte geboren wurde, kurz nachdem Mrs. Otis von einer Reise nach Athen zurückgekehrt war."

Lord Canterville hörte der langen Rede des würdigen Gesandten aufmerksam

his grey moustache now and then to hide an involuntary smile, and when Mr. Otis had ended, he shook him cordially by the hand, and said: "My dear sir, your charming little daughter rendered my unlucky ancestor, Sir Simon, a very important service, and I and my family are much indebted to her for her marvellous courage and pluck.

The jewels are clearly hers, and, egad, I believe that if I were heartless enough to take them from her, the wicked old fellow would be out of his grave in a fortnight, leading me the devil of a life.

As for their being heirlooms, nothing is an heirloom that is not so mentioned in a will or legal document, and the existence of these jewels has been quite unknown.

I assure you I have no more claim on them than your butler, and when Miss Virginia grows up, I dare say she will be pleased to have pretty things to wear.

Besides, you forget, Mr. Otis, that you took the furniture and the ghost at a valuation, and anything that belonged to the ghost passed at once into your possession, as, whatever activity Sir Simon may have shown in the corridor at night, in point of law he was really dead, and you acquired his property by purchase."

zu, während er sich ab und zu den langen grauen Schnurrbart strich, um ein unwillkürliches Lächeln zu verbergen; und als Mr. Otis schwieg, schüttelte er ihm herzlich die Hand und sagte: „Mein lieber Mr. Otis, Ihre entzückende kleine Tochter bat meinem unglücklichen Vorfahren, Sir Simon, einen höchst wichtigen Dienst geleistet, und meine Familie und ich sind ihr für den bewiesenen erstaunlichen Mut zu sehr großem Dank verpflichtet.

Ganz zweifellos sind die Juwelen Miss Virginias Eigentum; und wahrhaftig, ich glaube, wäre ich herzlos genug, sie ihr fortzunehmen, der böse alte Bursche würde noch diese Woche wieder aus seinem Grabe aufstehen und mir das Leben hier zur Hölle machen.

Und was den Begriff Erbstück anbelangt, so ist nichts ein Erbstück, was nicht mit diesem Ausdruck in einem Testament oder sonst einem rechtskräftigen Schriftstück also bezeichnet ist, und von der Existenz dieser Juwelen ist nichts bekannt gewesen.

Ich versichere Sie, dass ich nicht mehr Anspruch auf sie habe als Ihr Kammerdiener, und wenn Miss Virginia erwachsen ist, so wird sie, meine ich, doch ganz gern solche hübschen Sachen tragen.

Außerdem vergessen Sie ganz, Mr. Otis, dass Sie ja damals die ganze Einrichtung und das Gespenst mit dazu übernommen haben, und alles, was zu dem Besitztum des Gespenstes gehörte, wurde damit Ihr Eigentum; und was auch Sir Simon für eine merkwürdige Tätigkeit nachts auf dem Korridor entfaltet haben mag, vom Standpunkt des Gesetzes aus war er absolut tot, und somit erwarben Sie durch Kauf sein Eigentum.“

Mr. Otis was a good deal distressed at Lord Canterville's refusal, and begged him to reconsider his decision, but the good-natured peer was quite firm, and finally induced the Minister to allow his daughter to retain the present the ghost had given her, and when, in the spring of 1890, the young Duchess of Cheshire was presented at the Queen's first drawing-room on the occasion of her marriage, her jewels were the universal theme of admiration.

For Virginia received the coronet, which is the reward of all good little American girls, and was married to her boy-lover as soon as he came of age.

They were both so charming, and they loved each other so much, that every one was delighted at the match, except the old Marchioness of Dumbleton, who had tried to catch the Duke for one of her seven unmarried daughters, and had given no less than three expensive dinner-parties for that purpose, and, strange to say, Mr. Otis himself.

Mr. Otis was extremely fond of the young Duke personally, but, theoretically, he objected to titles, and, to use his own words, "was not without apprehension lest, amid the enervating influences of a pleasure-loving aristocracy, the true principles of Republican simplicity should be forgotten."

His objections, however, were completely overruled, and I believe that when he walked up the aisle of St. George's, Hanover Square, with his daughter leaning on his arm, there was

Mr. Otis war anfangs wirklich verstimmt, dass Lord Canterville auf sein Verlangen nicht eingehen wollte, und bat ihn, seine Entscheidung nochmals zu überlegen; aber der gutmütige Lord war fest entschlossen und überredete schließlich den Gesandten, seiner Tochter doch zu erlauben, das Geschenk des Gespenstes zu behalten; und als im Frühjahr 1890 die junge Herzogin von Cheshire bei Gelegenheit ihrer Hochzeit bei Hofe vorgestellt wurde, erregten ihre Juwelen die allgemeine Bewunderung.

Denn Virginia bekam wirklich und tatsächlich eine Krone in ihr Wappen, was die Belohnung für alle braven kleinen Amerikanerinnen ist, und heiratete ihren jugendlichen Bewerber, sobald sie mündig geworden war.

Sie waren ein so entzückendes Paar und liebten einander so sehr, dass jeder sich über die Heirat freute, jeder außer der Herzogin von Dumbleton — die den jungen Herzog gern für eine ihrer sieben unverheirateten Töchter gekapert hätte und nicht weniger als drei sehr teure Diners zu dem Zweck gegeben hatte — und wunderbarerweise auch außer Mr. Otis selber.

Mr. Otis hatte den jungen Herzog persönlich sehr gern, aber in der Theorie waren ihm alle Titel zuwider, und ‚er war', um seine eigenen Worte zu gebrauchen, ‚nicht ohne Besorgnis, dass inmitten der entnervenden Einflüsse der vergnügungssüchtigen englischen Aristokratie die einzig wahren Grundsätze republikanischer Einfachheit vergessen werden würden'.

Sein Widerstand wurde jedoch völlig besiegt, und ich glaube, dass es, als er in St. Georges Hanover Square mit seiner Tochter am Arm durch die Kirche schritt, keinen stolzeren Mann in ganz

not a prouder man in the whole length and breadth of England.

The Duke and Duchess, after the honeymoon was over, went down to Canterville Chase, and on the day after their arrival they walked over in the afternoon to the lonely churchyard by the pine-woods.

There had been a great deal of difficulty at first about the inscription on Sir Simon's tombstone, but finally it had been decided to engrave on it simply the initials of the old gentleman's name, and the verse from the library window.

The Duchess had brought with her some lovely roses, which she strewed upon the grave, and after they had stood by it for some time they strolled into the ruined chancel of the old abbey.

There the Duchess sat down on a fallen pillar, while her husband lay at her feet smoking a cigarette and looking up at her beautiful eyes.

Suddenly he threw his cigarette away, took hold of her hand, and said to her, "Virginia, a wife should have no secrets from her husband."

"Dear Cecil!

I have no secrets from you."

"Yes, you have," he answered, smiling, "you have never told me what happened to you when you were locked up with the ghost."

"I have never told any one, Cecil," said Virginia, gravely.

"I know that, but you might tell me."

"Please don't ask me, Cecil, I cannot tell you.

England gab als ihn.

Der Herzog und seine junge Frau kamen nach den Flitterwochen auf Schloss Canterville, und am Tage nach ihrer Ankunft gingen sie des Nachmittags zu dem kleinen einsamen Friedhof unter den Tannen.

Man hatte erst über die Inschrift auf Sir Simons Grabstein nicht schlüssig werden können und nach vielen Schwierigkeiten war dann entschieden worden, nur die Initialen seines Namens und den Vers vom Fenster der Bibliothek eingravieren zu lassen.

Die Herzogin hatte wundervolle Rosen mitgebracht, die sie auf das Grab streute, und nachdem sie eine Zeitlang stillgestanden hatten, schlenderten sie weiter zu der halbverfallenen Kanzel in der alten Abtei.

Dort setzte sich Virginia auf eine der umgestürzten Säulen; ihr Mann legte sich ihr zu Füßen in das Gras, rauchte eine Zigarette und blickte ihr verliebt und glücklich in die schönen Augen.

Plötzlich warf er seine Zigarette fort, ergriff ihre Hand und sagte: „Virginia, eine Frau sollte keine Geheimnisse vor ihrem Mann haben !“

„Aber lieber Cecil!

Ich habe doch keine Geheimnisse vor dir.“

„Doch, das hast du“, antwortete er lächelnd, „du hast mir nie gesagt, was dir begegnet ist, als du mit dem Gespenst verschwunden warst.“

„Das habe ich niemandem gesagt“, sagte Virginia ernst.

„Das weiß ich, aber du könntest es mir jetzt doch sagen.“

„Bitte, verlange das nicht von mir, Cecil, denn ich kann es dir nicht sagen ...

Poor Sir Simon! I owe him a great deal.	Der arme Sir Simon! Ich bin ihm zu so großem Danke verpflichtet.
Yes, don't laugh, Cecil, I really do.	Ja, da brauchst du nicht zu lachen, Cecil, es ist wirklich wahr.
He made me see what Life is, and what Death signifies, and why Love is stronger than both."	Er hat mich einsehen gelehrt, was das Leben ist und was der Tod bedeutet und warum die Liebe stärker ist als beide zusammen."
The Duke rose and kissed his wife lovingly.	Der Herzog stand auf und küsste seine junge Frau sehr zärtlich.
"You can have your secret as long as I have your heart," he murmured.	„Du kannst dein Geheimnis behalten, solange mir nur dein Herz gehört", sagte er leise.
"You have always had that, Cecil."	„Das Herz hat dir schon immer gehört, Cecil."
"And you will tell our children some day, won't you?"	„Aber unsern Kindern wirst du einst dein Geheimnis sagen, nicht wahr?"
Virginia blushed.	Virginia errötete.

Please send an email to **bonus@forum-sprachen-lernen.com** with the subject "**Canterville En-De**" to receive:

- **a download link for a free audiobook**

- **the Anki Deck for learning the most important vocabulary**.

We will not pass on your contact information to a third party.

The audiobook helps you to listen to the story repeatedly. **This way, you quickly enhance your listening comprehension, pronunciation as well as expand the vocabulary on the go**.

You liked the book, and it proved helpful? Please provide us with feedback; it would be much appreciated. Even if your review is comprised of just one or two sentences, it would help us tremendously.

If you want to further improve your language skills, other books using the same alignment are:

English – French:

The Picture of Dorian Gray **(with Audio)** (Mystery, Psychological Thriller)

The Snow Queen **(with Audio)** (Fairy Tale by H.C. Andersen)

French Short Stories **(with Audio)** Short Stories by Edgar Allan Poe

The Speckled Band **(with Audio)** A Sherlock Holmes Story

English – German:

The Red-Headed League (A Sherlock Holmes mystery)

Alice in Wonderland (Children's classic book)

The Wonderful Adventures of Nils (Adventure of Nils Holgersson with the wild geese)

The Snow Queen (Fairy Tale by H.C. Andersen)

The Picture of Dorian Gray **(with Audio)** (Mystery, Psychological Thriller)

A Christmas Carol (Classic world literature by Charles Dickens)

German Short Stories **(with Audio)** Short Stories by Edgar Allan Poe

English – Italian

Alice in Wonderland (Children's classic book)

Manufactured by Amazon.ca
Acheson, AB

11115493R00037